THE
NEZ PERCE

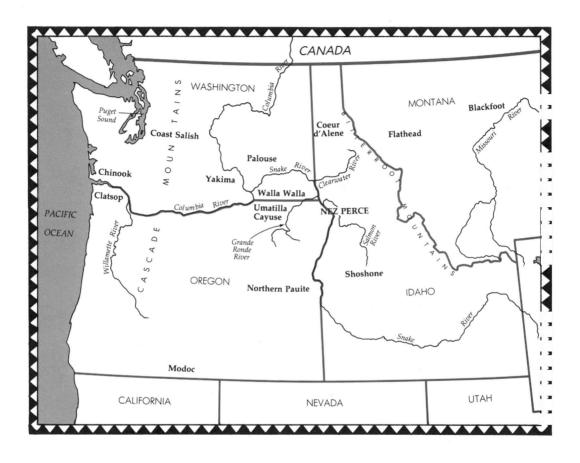

INDIANS OF NORTH AMERICA

THE
NEZ PERCE

Clifford E. Trafzer
University of California, Riverside

Frank W. Porter III
General Editor

CHELSEA HOUSE PUBLISHERS
New York   Philadelphia

On the cover A late-19th-century martingale made of buckskin and woolen cloth and decorated with blue, yellow, and white beads. The Nez Perce tied martingales around the necks of their horses during ceremonial occasions.

Chelsea House Publishers
Editor-in-Chief Remmel Nunn
Managing Editor Karyn Gullen Browne
Copy Chief Mark Rifkin
Picture Editor Adrian G. Allen
Art Director Maria Epes
Assistant Art Director Howard Brotman
Manufacturing Director Gerald Levine
Systems Manager Lindsey Ottman
Production Manager Joseph Romano
Production Coordinator Marie Claire Cebrián

Indians of North America
Senior Editor Liz Sonneborn

Staff for **THE NEZ PERCE**
Copy Editor Christopher Duffy
Editorial Assistant Michele Berezansky
Designer Debora Smith
Picture Researcher Melanie Sanford

First Printing

1 3 5 7 9 8 6 4 2

Library of Congress Cataloging-in-Publication Data

Trafzer, Clifford E.
The Nez Perce/by Clifford E. Trafzer.
  p. cm.—(Indians of North America)
Includes bibliographical references and index.
Summary: Examines the history, culture, and changing fortunes of the Nez Perce Indians. Includes a picture essay on their crafts.
ISBN 1-55546-720-2
    0-7910-0391-4 (pbk.)
1. Nez Perce Indians. [1. Nez Perce Indians. 2. Indians of North America.] I. Title II. Series: Indians of North America (Chelsea House Publishers)
                                                     91-25407
E99.N5T7 1991   CIP
973'.04974—dc20   AC

CONTENTS

INDIANS OF NORTH AMERICA

CHELSEA HOUSE PUBLISHERS

INDIANS OF NORTH AMERICA: CONFLICT AND SURVIVAL

Frank W. Porter III

The Indians survived our open intention of wiping them out, and since the tide turned they have even weathered our good intentions toward them, which can be much more deadly.

John Steinbeck
America and Americans

When Europeans first reached the North American continent, they found hundreds of tribes occupying a vast and rich country. The newcomers quickly recognized the wealth of natural resources. They were not, however, so quick or willing to recognize the spiritual, cultural, and intellectual riches of the people they called Indians.

The Indians of North America examines the problems that develop when people with different cultures come together. For American Indians, the consequences of their interaction with non-Indian people have been both productive and tragic. The Europeans believed they had "discovered" a "New World," but their religious bigotry, cultural bias, and materialistic world view kept them from appreciating and understanding the people who lived in it. All too often they attempted to change the way of life of the indigenous people. The Spanish conquistadores wanted the Indians as a source of labor. The Christian missionaries, many of whom were English, viewed them as potential converts. French traders and trappers used the Indians as a means to obtain pelts. As Francis Parkman, the 19th-century historian, stated, "Spanish civilization crushed the Indian; English civilization scorned and neglected him; French civilization embraced and cherished him."

7

Nearly 500 years later, many people think of American Indians as curious vestiges of a distant past, waging a futile war to survive in a Space Age society. Even today, our understanding of the history and culture of American Indians is too often derived from unsympathetic, culturally biased, and inaccurate reports. The American Indian, described and portrayed in thousands of movies, television programs, books, articles, and government studies, has either been raised to the status of the "noble savage" or disparaged as the "wild Indian" who resisted the westward expansion of the American frontier.

Where in this popular view are the real Indians, the human beings and communities whose ancestors can be traced back to ice-age hunters? Where are the creative and indomitable people whose sophisticated technologies used the natural resources to ensure their survival, whose military skill might even have prevented European settlement of North America if not for devastating epidemics and disruption of the ecology? Where are the men and women who are today diligently struggling to assert their legal rights and express once again the value of their heritage?

The various Indian tribes of North America, like people everywhere, have a history that includes population expansion, adaptation to a range of regional environments, trade across wide networks, internal strife, and warfare. This was the reality. Europeans justified their conquests, however, by creating a mythical image of the New World and its native people. In this myth, the New World was a virgin land, waiting for the Europeans. The arrival of Christopher Columbus ended a timeless primitiveness for the original inhabitants.

Also part of this myth was the debate over the origins of the American Indians. Fantastic and diverse answers were proposed by the early explorers, missionairies, and settlers. Some thought that the Indians were descended from the Ten Lost Tribes of Israel, others that they were descended from inhabitants of the lost continent of Atlantis. One writer suggested that the Indians had reached North America in another Noah's ark.

A later myth, perpetrated by many historians, focused on the relentless persecution during the past five centuries until only a scattering of these "primitive" people remained to be herded onto reservations. This view fails to chronicle the overt and covert ways in which the Indians successfully coped with the intruders.

All of these myths presented one-sided interpretations that ignored the complexity of European and American events and policies. All left serious questions unanswered. What were the origins of the American Indians? Where did they come from? How and when did they get to the New World? What was their life—their culture—really like?

In the late 1800s, anthropologists and archaeologists in the Smithsonian Institution's newly created Bureau of American Ethnology in Washington,

D.C., began to study scientifically the history and culture of the Indians of North America. They were motivated by an honest belief that the Indians were on the verge of extinction and that along with them would vanish their languages, religious beliefs, technology, myths, and legends. These men and women went out to visit, study, and record data from as many Indian communities as possible before this information was forever lost.

By this time there was a new myth in the national consciousness. American Indians existed as figures in the American past. They had performed a historical mission. They had challenged white settlers who trekked across the continent. Once conquered, however, they were supposed to accept graciously the way of life of their conquerors.

The reality again was different. American Indians resisted both actively and passively. They refused to lose their unique identity, to be assimilated into white society. Many whites viewed the Indians not only as members of a conquered nation but also as "inferior" and "unequal." The rights of the Indians could be expanded, contracted, or modified as the conquerors saw fit. In every generation, white society asked itself what to do with the American Indians. Their answers have resulted in the twists and turns of federal Indian policy.

There were two general approaches. One way was to raise the Indians to a "higher level" by "civilizing" them. Zealous missionaries considered it their Christian duty to elevate the Indian through conversion and scanty education. The other approach was to ignore the Indians until they disappeared under pressure from the ever-expanding white society. The myth of the "vanishing Indian" gave stronger support to the latter option, helping to justify the taking of the Indians' land.

Prior to the end of the 18th century, there was no national policy on Indians simply because the American nation had not yet come into existence. American Indians similarly did not possess a political or social unity with which to confront the various Europeans. They were not homogeneous. Rather, they were loosely formed bands and tribes, speaking nearly 300 languages and thousands of dialects. The collective identity felt by Indians today is a result of their common experiences of defeat and/or mistreatment at the hands of whites.

During the colonial period, the British crown did not have a coordinated policy toward the Indians of North America. Specific tribes (most notably the Iroquois and the Cherokee) became military and political pawns used by both the crown and the individual colonies. The success of the American Revolution brought no immediate change. When the United States acquired new territory from France and Mexico in the early 19th century, the federal government wanted to open this land to settlement by homesteaders. But the Indian tribes that lived on this land had signed treaties with European governments assuring their title to the land. Now the United States assumed legal responsibility for honoring these treaties.

At first, President Thomas Jefferson believed that the Louisiana Purchase contained sufficient land for both the Indians and the white population. Within a generation, though, it became clear that the Indians would not be allowed to remain. In the 1830s the federal government began to coerce the eastern tribes to sign treaties agreeing to relinquish their ancestral land and move west of the Mississippi River. Whenever these negotiations failed, President Andrew Jackson used the military to remove the Indians. The southeastern tribes, promised food and transportation during their removal to the West, were instead forced to walk the "Trail of Tears." More than 4,000 men, woman, and children died during this forced march. The "removal policy" was successful in opening the land to homesteaders, but it created enormous hardships for the Indians.

By 1871 most of the tribes in the United States had signed treaties ceding most or all of their ancestral land in exchange for reservations and welfare. The treaty terms were intended to bind both parties for all time. But in the General Allotment Act of 1887, the federal government changed its policy again. Now the goal was to make tribal members into individual landowners and farmers, encouraging their absorption into white society. This policy was advantageous to whites who were eager to acquire Indian land, but it proved disastrous for the Indians. One hundred thirty-eight million acres of reservation land were subdivided into tracts of 160, 80, or as little as 40 acres, and allotted tribe members on an individual basis. Land owned in this way was said to have "trust status" and could not be sold. But the surplus land—all Indian land not allotted to individuals—was opened (for sale) to white settlers. Ultimately, more than 90 million acres of land were taken from the Indians by legal and illegal means.

The resulting loss of land was a catastrophe for the Indians. It was necessary to make it illegal for Indians to sell their land to non-Indians. The Indian Reorganization Act of 1934 officially ended the allotment period. Tribes that voted to accept the provisions of this act were reorganized, and an effort was made to purchase land within preexisting reservations to restore an adequate land base.

Ten years later, in 1944, federal Indian policy again shifted. Now the federal government wanted to get out of the "Indian business." In 1953 an act of Congress named specific tribes whose trust status was to be ended "at the earliest possible time." This new law enabled the United States to end unilaterally, whether the Indians wished it or not, the special status that protected the land in Indian tribal reservations. In the 1950s federal Indian policy was to transfer federal responsibility and jurisdiction to state governments, encourage the physical relocation of Indian peoples from reservations to urban areas, and hasten the termination, or extinction, of tribes.

Between 1954 and 1962 Congress passed specific laws authorizing the termination of more than 100 tribal groups. The stated purpose of the termination policy was to ensure the full and complete integration of Indians into American society. However, there is a less benign way to interpret this legislation. Even as termination was being discussed in Congress, 133 separate bills were introduced to permit the transfer of trust land ownership from Indians to non-Indians.

With the Johnson administration in the 1960s the federal government began to reject termination. In the 1970s yet another Indian policy emerged. Known as "self-determination," it favored keeping the protective role of the federal government while increasing tribal participation in, and control of, important areas of local government. In 1983 President Reagan, in a policy statement on Indian affairs, restated the unique "government is government" relationship of the United States with the Indians. However, federal programs since then have moved toward transferring Indian affairs to individual states, which have long desired to gain control of Indian land and resources.

As long as American Indians retain power, land, and resources that are coveted by the states and the federal government, there will continue to be a "clash of cultures," and the issues will be contested in the courts, Congress, the White House, and even in the international human rights community. To give all Americans a greater comprehension of the issues and conflicts involving American Indians today is a major goal of this series. These issues are not easily understood, nor can these conflicts be readily resolved. The study of North American Indian history and culture is a necessary and important step toward that comprehension. All Americans must learn the history of the relations between the Indians and the federal government, recognize the unique legal status of the Indians, and understand the heritage and cultures of the Indians of North America.

This medallion was found during an excavation of Nez Perce burial sites on the Snake River near present-day Lewiston, Idaho. Made especially for the Lewis and Clark expedition, such medals were presented by the explorers to the leaders of each tribe they encountered.

MEETING
THE
EXPLORERS

In September 1805, a ragtag band of American explorers forged westward across a steep, rocky, and forested trail. They were exhausted, having crossed the rugged Lolo Pass through the Bitterroot Mountains from present-day Montana into Idaho. President Thomas Jefferson had dispatched these men under the leadership of William Clark and Meriwether Lewis to lay claim to and explore the lands west of the Mississippi River. The president had also sent this group, known as the Corps of Discovery, to map and record their journey to the Pacific Ocean.

As the explorers neared the western end of the Lolo Trail, they split into two groups. Lewis and his men stayed in the woods. Clark and his group moved forward. Within a short time, Clark's company rode out of the forest onto a wide plain later known as the Weippe Prairie. The group pushed across the open prairie, which was dotted here and there with groves of pine trees and low-lying shrubs. From their vantage point high on the plain, the men spotted Indian dwellings. They then rode toward the A-framed lodges and scattered tipis to meet their inhabitants, the Indians who called themselves the Nee Mee Poo. (In his journals, Clark would call this tribe the Chopunish. They are now better known as the Nez Perce, which is French for "pierced nose.")

Three Nez Perce boys slowly approached the white men but ran into the bushes when they saw their bearded faces. These young people had heard of the *suyapo*, or white men, but they had never met any. According to some accounts, the first white man encountered by northwestern Indians was bearded and bald. The Indians called that person suyapo, meaning head upside down. Fearing an attack by the suyapo, the boys hid from Clark and his men.

Not wishing to alarm the Indians, Clark disarmed himself and dismounted. He walked into the tall grass and found two of the boys. Clark gave them gifts and told them in sign language that he had come in peace. The explorer and his men then entered the village of Broken Arm, a great war chief. He was away at the time, leading a war party against the Shoshone Indians.

The village's male and female elders and a group of children led Clark into Broken Arm's tipi. There the Americans were treated to a feast of buffalo, salmon, and camas roots. Children watched the strangers' every move, struggling to get a good look at the newcomers. Soon after, Clark continued his journey to another nearby Nez Perce village, where he met Chief Walammottinin (Hair Bunched and Tied). More often, this leader was simply called Twisted Hair.

At both villages, the Nez Perce treated Clark and his men with respect and kindness. Realizing that they were a friendly tribe, Clark sent one of his men back to the Lolo Trail to lead Lewis into the village. This group met no hostility from the Nez Perce, either, because, in part, of the experiences of an elderly woman named Watkuweis (Returned from a Far Country). Many years before, she had been captured by Blackfeet, or Atsina Indians, who traded her to Canadian trappers. The trappers eventually returned her to the Nez Perce. When Lewis and Clark arrived, Watkuweis told her tribe, "These are the people who helped me," and urged her people not to attack the white men.

Although Twisted Hair and others may have been influenced by Watkuweis, they had another reason for welcoming the Americans. Few Nez Perce

Meriwether Lewis was serving as Thomas Jefferson's private secretary when, in 1804, the president asked him and his close friend William Clark to explore the vast tract the United States had acquired through the Louisiana Purchase the previous year. Their journals provided eastern Americans with the first detailed information about the people and lands west of the Mississippi River.

had ever met the suyapo, but they knew from other Indians that whites brought with them a variety of useful items, such as guns, powder, lead, knives, pots, cloth, and beads. A desire to trade for these goods led some Indians to cultivate friendships with the whites.

The Indians did not perceive the white men as a threat to their security. The explorers showed no sign of wanting war and were traveling with a young Shoshone woman named Sacagawea and her baby boy. Because Indian war parties generally did not include women and children, the Nez Perce believed that Lewis and Clark meant them no harm. The Indians were correct in their assessment. Lewis and Clark desired friendly relations with the Nez Perce because they hoped the Indians could help them reach the Pacific Ocean and then return home.

In their discussions with the Indians, the explorers recognized that the Nez Perce's language, Sahaptin, was different from the Interior Salish tongue of the Flathead Indians, whom the white men had met in Montana. To some extent, they could communicate with the Indians through sign language. However, a great deal of what was said by each group became lost in the process.

When Lewis and Clark told the Indians they wanted to travel to the ocean, Twisted Hair used charcoal to draw a map on the smooth side of an elk hide. Following the directions on the map, the explorers could travel by

From his experiences during the Lewis and Clark expedition, William Clark developed a great respect for Indian cultures. Years later, while serving as superintendent of Indian affairs, he helped create federal policies relating to western Indians.

canoe from the lands of the Nez Perce to the Pacific Ocean. In order to make the journey west, the explorers needed boats. Twisted Hair and his sons helped the explorers locate a boat-building camp on the Clearwater River, and they showed them how the Nez Perce constructed canoes from cedar.

The Indians and whites worked side by side cutting down huge cedar trees.

At first, the explorers tried to make dugout canoes using their small axes. When this proved to be a slow process, Twisted Hair and his people taught the Americans how to burn the middle of the logs before digging out the wood. The whites adopted the Indian way and eventually finished 5 boats in 10 days. Twisted Hair, Tetoharsky, and other Nez Perce joined the expedition. The Indians were familiar with the river and warned the explorers of such dangers as sandbars and rapids. The Nez Perce scouts may even have saved the Americans' life.

Lewis and Clark showed their appreciation by giving gifts—including cloth, tobacco, beads, flags, and ribbons—to the Indian leaders. The explorers also handed out special medals struck for the expedition. Each medal looked like a large coin: On one side was a likeness of President Jefferson, and on the other was a long-stemmed Indian pipe and a tomahawk. Under the symbol were the words *Peace and Friendship*. The Nez Perce treasured these medals throughout the next century, passing on to their children the story of the coming of Lewis and Clark. Sometimes they displayed the medals to visitors, and today one of them is preserved by the Nez Perce Tribe of Idaho.

Before leaving Nez Perce territory, Lewis and Clark learned many things about the people. They noted that the Nez Perce had a dynamic culture that changed with the world around them. For many years, the Nez Perce had traveled into present-day Montana, Idaho, and Wyoming to hunt buffalo. A special buffalo-hunting class emerged in Nez Perce society. Sometimes groups from this class would remain on the hunt in the Great Plains for two or three years. In time, the Nez Perce adopted some of the customs of the Plains Indians that the hunters encountered. These borrowed cultural characteristics included tipis, eagle headdresses, art designs, and music.

On the plateau, the Nez Perce generally had peaceful relations with their Interior Salish–speaking neighbors to the north and their Sahaptin-speaking relatives to the west. But the Nez Perce also had enemies. After 1750, when the tribe began to trade with other Indians for horses, warfare between tribes increased because the speed of travel on horseback made it easier both to attack and to be attacked. The Nez Perce's greatest foes were the Shoshone and the Blackfeet. (Shortly after Lewis and Clark left Nez Perce country, Broken Arm returned to his village with 42 Shoshone scalps he had taken in retaliation for the Shoshone's killing of 3 Nez Perces.) According to Lewis and Clark's journals, all of the Indians in the Northwest considered the Nez Perce a powerful people.

The explorers had arrived in the Nez Perce homeland in Pekhoonmaikahl, the time when the fall salmon swim upriver and when the fingerlings journey downstream to the ocean. When Lewis and Clark left the region, it was Hopelul, the time when the tamarack

A Nez Perce camp on the Yellowstone River in present-day Montana, photographed by W. H. Jackson in 1871. After the Nez Perce acquired horses in the 18th century, their hunters began to travel to the Great Plains to stalk buffalo. From the Plains Indians they met, they borrowed many cultural characteristics, such as constructing buffalo-skin tipis.

trees turn yellow. These were important times for the people, as they were busy storing food and fuel for the winter. The women and children gathered, dried, and stored roots and berries. The men fished for salmon using hooks, nets, spears, and traps. With bows and arrows they also hunted deer, elk, and bear.

The autumn was also the time of year when young girls and boys sought their *wyakin*, or guardian spirit power. Usually parents and grandparents would prepare young people for this experience. When the children reached the age of 10 or 11, family elders took them to a sacred spot and left them alone. They could drink all the water they wanted, but they could not eat.

During the vigil their spirit power would come to them, revealing truths about their life and often teaching them special songs. The vision might appear as blue mist, a water bug, a bear, or a buffalo. Boys and girls alike learned from their guardian spirits. They often shared their visions with elders, who helped them understand the power and what was expected of them. Throughout their life, the people might communicate with their wyakin and grow from the experience.

On his vigil, one young Nez Perce boy, who came to be known as Yellow Wolf, reported that "it was just like dreaming, what I saw." A form floated in front of him, saying, "My boy, look at me! You do as I am telling you, and you will be as I am. Take a good look at me! I will give you my power." The spirit was Hemene Moxmox, a wolf with yellow hair. "Like a human being," Yellow Wolf later remembered, "it talked to me, and gave me its power." The spirit gave the boy the ability to become a strong and effective warrior. Several times in his life, Hemene Moxmox taught the youth different lessons and gave him personal powers, or *somesh*. For example, Yellow Wolf learned how to find his people by instinct and how to detect an enemy close to his encampment. As an adult, the boy became a war chief who fought courageously during the worst war in Nez Perce history. He always credited his wyakin with his survival and success.

During the winter, the Nez Perce observed a medicine ceremony called the Wyakwatset. Young and old attended the ceremony, during which individuals encouraged each other to sing the songs taught to them by their guardian spirits. The people also danced in such a way as to imitate their wyakin. Sometimes they challenged each other to see who had the strongest spirit power. The winners often put other people into trances.

The Nez Perce held the medicine ceremony in large lodges called longhouses, which also served as winter dwellings for extended families. During the long months of snow, wind, and ice, children gathered around their elders to hear stories. Known as oral tradition, this practice of storytelling was an important part of the history, religion, literature, and culture of the people. Today the Nez Perce still share these stories, which explain a great deal about the people. The stories describe the beginning of time and the creation of the plants, animals, rivers, and mountains. From them, children learn that everything on earth has a soul and being, that everything is interrelated, and that the Nez Perce owe much to the teachings of Coyote, the trickster. Coyote did not always do the right thing, but people learned from his errors as well as his successes.

According to Nez Perce beliefs, at the beginning of time, Coyote traveled about free and without a care. He did so until "an enormous something that was named Iltswewitsix" began growing and eating everything in sight. The great being was also known as the Kamiah Monster. Nothing, it seemed, could stand against him.

Coyote knew that the monster would try to eat him, so he prepared for the meeting by tying himself to the earth. Coyote hoped that the monster would not find him and would pass him by without swallowing him. But the monster discovered the trickster and challenged him. He told Coyote to take in a deep breath and try to swallow him. Coyote tried, but he was able to move only one of the monster's legs. When the monster took his turn, he broke the bonds holding Coyote and pulled him near. Just as the monster was about to inhale Coyote, the trickster offered to jump inside the monster's body without a fight. Foolishly, the monster allowed Coyote to enter his body. Coyote walked directly to the monster's heart. He then built a fire, pulled out five knives he had concealed, and began to cut the heart. The monster pleaded with Coyote to come out, but he persisted. In the end, Coyote killed the monster and cut his body into many pieces, giving portions of the massive body to each group of people. After he had distributed all of the monster's body parts, Coyote realized that he had failed to save any portion for the Nez Perce people. He then decided to create the Nez Perce from the life-giving blood of the monster, which became their source of strength, courage, and honor.

On their way to the Pacific Ocean, Lewis and Clark passed a hill along the Clearwater River that is said to be the Kamiah Monster's heart. They moved swiftly westward to the junction of the Clearwater and Snake rivers, continuing on through the lands of the Palouse Indians. The Snake River flowed into the Columbia River at a place called Quosispah, a Palouse village and tra-

This hill, located southeast of Kamiah, Idaho, is revered by the Nez Perce as the place of their creation. According to legend, the land formation is the heart of the Kamiah Monster, from whose blood the Nez Perce were formed.

A late-19th-century photograph of a boy named A-kis-kis, with his Nez Perce father, Jo A-kis-kis, and Palouse mother, Hal-a-mis. Traditionally, Nez Perce men, women, and children all worked together to obtain food from their abundant environment for their families.

ditional meeting area for Indians traveling to different places. The Nez Perce who had accompanied the explorers journeyed as far as Quosispah before returning home. The Corps of Discovery then continued down the Columbia River to the lands of the Chinook and the Clatsop Indians. There they spent a cold, dreary winter.

While Lewis and Clark wintered at Fort Clatsop, the Nez Perce lived in their lodges along the Clearwater,

Salmon, Snake, Grande Ronde, and tributaries of these great rivers. During the first months of winter, the Nez Perce lived comfortably off the bounty of roots, fish, berries, venison, and waterfowl they had stored the previous year. But the winter of 1805–6 was fierce, with cold winds and deep snow. A food shortage resulted, and the Nez Perce had to venture out onto the Columbia Plateau to hunt for fresh food, but they found little. Nevertheless, they survived and spent the rest of the winter weaving baskets, making clothing, repairing hunting gear, making fishing tackle, and sharing stories.

In Lahtetahl, the time when flowers began to blossom, the Nez Perce men rounded up the horses and began breaking them. Women and children then mounted the spirited animals and, with the men, started their seasonal round to the root fields. The snow was still deep, but some bands moved out in March and April to gather early roots. They worked the root grounds until June, when the salmon started to swim upriver. Then they returned to their permanent homes along the rivers to fish and hold their first salmon ceremonies. For the Nez Perce, catching and eating salmon was a spiritual activity, part of their religion. Their spiritual beliefs still require that they eat salmon and drink water in communion with the Creator each year.

While the Nez Perce fished and gathered, Lewis and Clark made their way east to the villages of Twisted Hair, Tetoharsky, Broken Arm, and others. The Americans were pleased when Twisted Hair returned the saddles, lead, flints, powder, and other goods the Corps of Discovery had left the previous fall. The explorers were even more elated to regain all of their horses, most of which were in good shape despite the harsh winter. Clearly, Twisted Hair and his people had done the explorers a great service. Through an interpreter, Lewis and Clark thanked the Indians for their many kindnesses, and the Indians held a huge council in honor of their white friends. The Americans handed out gifts, and the Indians did the same. They traded knives, blankets, kettles, and awls for scarce food. The two parties feasted, danced, and sang before ending their great meeting.

Deep drifts of pure white snow still blocked the Lolo Trail and prevented the Corps of Discovery from crossing the Bitterroot Mountains. Thus, the explorers lived among the Nez Perce until the middle of June, when they began their difficult journey through the steep, rocky forests on the western slopes of the mountains. The Americans were again aided in their travels by three Nez Perce scouts who knew the Lolo Trail and guided them safely over the pass. By the end of the month, the explorers soaked their aching muscles in the soothing waters of the Lolo Hot Springs. They crossed the dangerous mountains, entered the Bitterroot Valley of present-day Montana, and prepared themselves to face the hazards of the Rocky Mountains.

Before leaving the region, Lewis had made an entry in his journal, commenting that "this country would form an extensive settlement." The value of the land and its resources west of the Bitterroots was not lost on him or the other members of the Corps of Discovery. Lewis could already envision a time when white families would settle on lands that had once been the sole domain of the Indians, something the Nez Perce could little imagine. ▲

The Nez Perce were renowned as skilled horse trainers. Mounted on horses, they were able to travel long distances to trade with other Indian groups and with the non-Indian traders who arrived in the West in the 19th century.

THE
INDIAN
TRADE

The Nez Perce and their neighbors had been involved in trade long before the arrival of Europeans. To the east, they traded with the Crow, the Flathead, and the Sioux. To the west, their trading partners were the Palouse, the Walla Walla, and the Chinook. Among the goods exchanged for canoes, hides, and flints were horses, well-crafted bows, parfleches (rawhide bags that resembled large envelopes), and baskets.

The arrival of Lewis and Clark brought new economic prospects for the Nez Perce. For the first time, they were able to obtain guns, ammunition, knives, fishhooks, pots, pans, and other non-Indian goods. Before leaving, the explorers assured the Indians more Americans would come to trade with them. But the Nez Perce's first opportunity to trade for manufactured items on a large scale came not from the Americans but from the British.

The North West Company, a British-owned business, was the first major trading concern in the inland Pacific Northwest. David Thompson served as the head of this operation. Under his guidance, the company established four trading posts: Kootenay House, Kalispell House, Salish House, and Spokane House.

In July 1811, Thompson set off with a party of 10 down the Columbia River. In his journals, Thompson wrote that his mission was "to open a passage for the interior trade with the Pacific Ocean." The men traveled in a cedar canoe for six days. Finally, they arrived at the Palouse Indian village of Quosispah in present-day Washington State. The traders felt that this would be an excellent place for a trading factory. It was near the future site of Fort Nez Perces.

Thompson encountered many Indians living along the Columbia River but not the Nez Perce, who lived far to the east. He traveled to the mouth of the Columbia, where he met men employed by the Pacific Fur Company. These men worked for John Jacob Astor and were known as Astorians. Thompson then decided to return to the interior and begin sending furs downriver along the route he had traced. When his goods reached the Pacific Ocean, they would be shipped to Asia, where they could be sold at a great profit.

In his travels, Thompson became acquainted with David Stuart, an Astorian interested in learning more about the interior Northwest. While Thompson journeyed inland, Stuart met with a delegation of Indians at the mouth of the Walla Walla River. Among the Indians who attended this council were some Nez Perce. Alexander Ross, an Astorian, wrote that so many Indians attended the meeting that the Columbia Plain was "literally covered with horses, of which there could not have been less than four thousand in sight of camp." Ross described the grand scene:

> The men were generally tall, raw-boned, and well dressed; having all buffalo-robes, deer-skin leggings, very white, and most of them garnished with porcupine quills. Their shoes were also trimmed and painted red—

altogether, their appearance indicated wealth. Their voices were strong and masculine, and their language differed from any we had heard before. The women wore garments of well dressed deer-skin down to their heels; many of them richly garnished with beads . . . and other trinkets—leggings and shoes similar to those of the men. Their faces were painted red. On the whole, they differed widely in appearance from the . . . tribes we had seen along the river.

While Stuart met with the Nez Perce, the Palouse, the Walla Walla, the Cayuse, and other Indians assembed at the Walla Walla River, he noticed that the only manufactured goods they owned were a few guns, knives, and kettles. The Indians showed a great deal of interest in acquiring more items, and the traders were eager to supply them. They recognized that this region along the Columbia River would make an excellent trading center.

Meanwhile, another group of Astorians was traveling through the heart of the Nez Perce homeland. Wilson Price Hunt and his men had journeyed from St. Louis, Missouri, into present-day Idaho. The group had a difficult time traveling together, so they broke up into smaller bands. One group, led by Donald McKenzie, moved up the Snake River and through Hells Canyon. There they nearly starved to death. The men likely would have died without the help of the Nez Perce, who generously provided the trappers with food, medicine, and lodging. McKenzie left no de-

In 1811, New Yorker John Jacob Astor challenged the monopoly the British-owned North West Company had on the western fur trade by establishing Astoria, a large trading post at the mouth of the Columbia River. His employees, known as Astorians, were among the first non-Indians to trade with the Nez Perce.

The Nez Perce probably obtained these items—a brass powder flask, glass beads, a fire striker, and a dagger—from a Hudson's Bay Company trader in about 1820. Because Indians were eager to acquire manufactured goods, non-Indian traders thrived in the Northwest.

tailed record of this encounter, but it is known that when he recovered, he thanked his hosts and continued his travels. McKenzie and his party journeyed down the Snake River past the camps of some Nez Perce and Palouse. He reached Quosispah and continued on to Astoria, the trading post near the mouth of the Columbia founded by John Jacob Astor.

Along his trip, the Nez Perce had treated McKenzie with such hospitality that the businessman decided to set up a trading factory in their lands. With a group of Astorians he established a post in 1812, but business did not go as well as he had hoped. The Nez Perce thought that the prices McKenzie was asking were too high. Worse still, the Astorians accepted only furs—particularly beaver pelts—for their goods. The Nez Perce thought of hunting beavers as drudgery. According to Alexander Ross, the Nez Perce found it insulting that the whites wanted them to spend their days "crawling about in search of furs." Thus, the Indians effectively refused to trade with McKenzie.

The Astorians were also quite adamant, until they ran out of food. When McKenzie asked the Indians to sell him some food, the Indians demanded very high prices. McKenzie had to accept the terms outlined by the Indians, but he was not pleased.

In the fall of 1812, the Astorians hid their goods and traveled north to Spokane House. There they learned from their British counterparts that the United States and England were at war. As a result of this conflict—the War of 1812—the Astorians decided to leave the Northwest. The Astorians were outnumbered, and they worried that the British would press their claim to the region through armed conflict. McKenzie returned to Nez Perce country to retrieve his goods. When he arrived, he learned that the Indians had plundered his trading items. He recovered some of his possessions and bargained for some horses. Then he and his men rode west to the junction of the Walla Walla and Columbia rivers. There they learned that a fellow Astorian, John Clarke, had recklessly hanged a Palouse Indian at the village of Palus. The incident intensely angered the Indians, who were determined to have revenge.

Ross reported that the Indians who had grouped together in reaction to the hanging "could not have been less than two thousand, with a fleet of one hundred and seventy-four canoes along the beach." The Palouse, Cayuse, and Walla Walla composed the bulk of the Indians, but some Nez Perce warriors stood against the whites as well. The Palouse hanged by Clarke had friends among the Nez Perce. In addition, McKenzie had recently offended the Nez Perce. A delegation of Indian elders defused this hostile situation by meeting with the whites and negotiating a peace. The Astorians then moved north to Okanagan country and ultimately sold their interest in the region to the North West Company.

Some of the Astorians, including Ross Cox and Alexander Ross, remained in the region to work for the company. Both of these men lived through hostile encounters with Indians. For example, in May 1814, Ross attended a huge horse fair in the Yakima Valley, where Indian men and women met to trade horses. Some Wenatchi Indians had warned Ross not to go, but he ignored their advice. Ross later wrote that when he and his men arrived at the large camp, they "could see its beginning but not the end!" The "grand and imposing sight" included a camp 6 miles long filled with "3,000 men, exclusive of women and children, and treble that number of horses." The Indians surrounded the white men and would not allow them to leave for some time. The Indians could have easily killed the trappers, but they eventually chose to spare their lives.

The North West Company continued to operate on the Columbia Plateau in spite of minor hostilities. The Indians enjoyed the trade items, but they never permitted the whites to establish a permanent post in their territory. In 1818, the company decided to found a trading center "on a level point upon the east bank of the Columbia" that commanded "a spacious view of our noble stream in all its grandeur." The company named the post Fort Nez Perces, in honor of the great tribe. The whites did not know until later that they had built the post on lands claimed not by Nez Perce but by the Cayuse, the Palouse, and the Walla Walla.

The coat of arms of the Hudson's Bay Company. In 1825, the firm merged with the North West Company and gained control of Fort Nez Perces, (later renamed Fort Walla Walla).

In 1825, the North West Company merged with another trading firm, the Hudson's Bay Company. Eventually, company officials recognized their mistake in naming the post Fort Nez Perces. The new company changed the name to Fort Walla Walla, which became the "jumping off" place for Hudson's Bay trappers heading for the Rocky Mountains of Canada and the United States. The post commanded a significant site on the Columbia River and was important to the east-west movement of men and furs for the company. It also provided excellent horses for the trappers and goods for Indians throughout the area.

Many years before the arrival of Lewis and Clark, the Nez Perce had traveled to the Great Plains to hunt buffalo, fight their enemies, and trade. When American trappers began to have annual meetings there, the Nez Perce attended. Many of these Indians liked these mountain men, and became intrigued with the "power," or "medicine," of the whites. The Indians believed that all real power came from the Creator and was bestowed upon individuals by their wyakin. The manufactured goods of the whites seemed to be evidence of great power, and the Indians became interested in knowing more about this force. This curiosity eventually led some Nez Perce to seek greater knowledge of the source of the white people's power. ▲

Rabbit Skin Leggings, painted by George Catlin aboard a steamboat on the Missouri River in 1831, was one of four Nez Perces chosen by the tribe to travel to St. Louis, Missouri, to find out more about Christianity. The delegation's visit inspired several missionaries to journey west to attempt to convert the Nez Perce and their neighbors.

FAITHS, SPIRITS,
AND
MISSIONS

According to traditional Nez Perce beliefs, all living things were sacred. When the Creator formed life, he made the Law, which stipulated that humans should always give thanks to the earth, animals, and plants. The mountains, rivers, and rock formations also held special meaning to the Indians. Particularly revered were those sites where the young people went to seek their wy-akin.

The fur trappers generally did not try to influence the religious beliefs of the Nez Perce or their neighbors, even though some of the trappers were Christians. However, a few Indians demonstrated an interest in learning about the white people's religion. Two chiefs—Nicholas Garry, a Spokane Indian, and J. H. Pelly, a Flathead—sent their sons to the Red River settlement in Canada to be educated by Christian missionaries. In 1829, after four years

of instruction, the two men returned to their people to preach the gospel.

Word of their teachings reached the Nez Perce. In 1831, the tribe chose a delegation of four to travel to St. Louis, Missouri, to find out more about Christianity. Traveling with Lucien Fontenelle and Andrew Drips of the American Fur Company, the delegation reached the city and met with Bishop Joseph Rosati.

Two of the Nez Perce died of disease while in St. Louis, but the other two continued on, traveling up the Missouri River aboard the steamboat *Yellowstone*. Unfortunately, neither ever returned home. No Horns on His Head fell deathly ill on the boat, and Rabbit Skin Leggings was killed by Blackfoot Indians during a fight in Montana.

Despite the briefness of its visit, the Nez Perce delegation left quite an impression on Catholic and Protestant missionaries. This was largely due to an article written by Christian missionary G. P. Disoway that was published in the *Christian Advocate and Journal and Zion's Herald* about the "wandering sons of our native forest." Disoway's essay urged clergymen to convert the Nez Perce and establish missions in their territory.

In 1835, Marcus Whitman, a missionary from New York, responded by announcing his intention to convert Indians living in the Pacific Northwest. He requested a volunteer to help him and interviewed several candidates. Whitman chose Henry Harmon Spalding, a Presbyterian minister, to join in the venture. Before traveling west, Whitman married Narcissa Prentiss and Spalding married Eliza Hart because the American Board of Commissioners for Foreign Missions (the head office of all missionary efforts) required that male missionaries have a wife.

Accompanied by a fur trapper, Thomas Fitzpatrick, and a missionary, William H. Gray, the missionaries journeyed to the Northwest during the summer of 1836. En route, they met a group of Nez Perce who were hunting buffalo. The Indians guided them through present-day southern Idaho, across the Blue Mountains of present-day northeastern Oregon, and into the Walla Walla Valley. The Nez Perce left the missionaries in the care of Pierre C. Pambrun, the trader at Fort Walla Walla. In early September, the party traveled down the Columbia River to Fort Vancouver. Whitman established a mission at the Cayuse village of Waiilatpu, and Spalding did the same at Lapwai among the Nez Perce.

The missionaries' objective was to destroy the native religion and replace it with Protestant views, values, and ways. They considered Indian culture unworthy because they believed native beliefs were spawned by the devil. The missionaries challenged the authority of Indian holy people. According to historian Allen Slickpoo, Sr., the medicine people soon recognized the Christian missionaries were "demoralizing and weakening our cultural values, and ending our power and freedom so that we would be dependent on the whites."

Between 1836 and 1847, Spalding worked diligently among the Nez Perce. He preached about God and the devil, heaven and hell, and good and evil. The Indians responded to his teachings because they conformed to their own belief that religious leaders had both positive and negative powers. However, most Indians did not remain within the Christian fold. Many left after they witnessed Spalding's harsh dealings with nonbelievers. He whipped and abused them or directed pro-Christian Indians to do so.

Tensions increased after 1840, when several former fur trappers—including Joe Meek, Robert Newell, Caleb Wilkens, and William Craig—took their families in covered wagons through the Blue Mountains. They opened the Oregon Trail, providing a route for thousands of settlers to travel into the

Presbyterian missionary Henry Harmon Spalding arrived in Nez Perce country in 1836. Spalding's harsh treatment of Indians who did not want to become Christians soon instilled resentment in the tribe and eventually led some Nez Perce to resort to violence in order to force the minister to leave their territory.

Northwest. Today this trail is glorified by many people, but not by the Nez Perce or other Native Americans of the region. The Oregon Trail brought whites who took over lands that had

once been the sole home of Indians. These Americans brought diseases, such as smallpox, against which the Indians had no immunity. In 1846, a smallpox epidemic ravaged the Indian communities in the area. The next year, measles, another non-Indian disease, killed hundreds more Indian men, women, and children.

By 1847, many Nez Perce instructed the Spaldings to keep to themselves and stay out of Indian affairs. Other Indians told the zealous missionary to leave Nez Perce territory, but Spalding remained. To show their anger, a few Nez Perce broke the dam, fences, and windows at the mission. They used the fencing to build a huge fire and spent the evening singing loudly outside the minister's home. Outraged by their behavior, Spalding severely scolded the Indians. Their response caught the preacher by surprise. One of the Indians grabbed Spalding and wrestled him to the ground. The minister retreated to his home, where he wept all night. Still, he refused to heed the warning to leave.

Whitman had a similar experience among the Cayuse. The Indians came to resent the establishment of the Whitman mission on Indian land. When they asked Whitman to leave Waiilatpu, like Spalding, he refused.

Finally, some Indians resorted to violence to remove the missionaries from Indian lands. A few Cayuse rose against Whitman, killing him, Narcissa, and 11 others. At the time of the attack, Spalding was visiting the Walla Walla

A late-19th-century photograph of the bank of the Clearwater River, the location of the mission built by the Spaldings in the spring of 1838.

Valley. Warriors chased him across the plateau, and he barely reached Lapwai alive. Some Nez Perce had attacked Spalding's mission, but they had not harmed Eliza Spalding. Chief Big Thunder and his son-in-law, William Craig, rescued Eliza and kept her safe from the attackers. After this incident, Spalding left for a time, then continued to return and leave.

The result of the Whitman killings was war, waged by Oregon Territory's volunteer army against the Cayuse and Palouse Indians. The Nez Perce remained out of the fight, but they watched and learned. With the encouragement of Nez Perce leaders, five Cayuses eventually surrendered to Oregon officials. On June 3, 1850, the Americans hanged the five confessors,

also felt that the missionaries had laid a foundation for the destruction of their people by encouraging other whites to migrate to the Northwest. This development greatly concerned the Nez Perce, but their elders maintained that Indian prophets had foretold the coming of these new people. Old songs, still sung by the Nez Perce, tell of a people who would straighten out the crooked places of nature, seen as a reference to the building of railroads and highways. They also explained that these people would bring buffalo without beards, perhaps a reference to cattle, which were brought to North America by non-Indians.

Fur trappers and missionaries had certainly altered Nez Perce culture. But officials of the U.S. government soon caused even greater changes in the Indians' way of life. When settlers moved into the Willamette Valley, they demanded that the federal government relocate the Indians living there to lands east of the Cascade Mountains. They also asked the government to assert its authority over all Indians in the region. In 1842, Dr. Elijah White, who became the official in charge of the northwestern Indians, dictated a series of laws under which the Native Americans were to live. These laws meant little to the people, but they signaled that more demands on Indians would be forthcoming from the United States.

In 1853, the government split Oregon Territory into two sections. The northernmost was named Washington Territory and included most of present-

although only two had actually been involved.

As a result of the Spalding affair and the hanging of the Cayuse, an anti-Christian faction developed among the Indians of the Northwest. These Indians harbored great resentment toward Christians. As one Nez Perce explained: "We were demoralized by the ministers of Christianity. We were soon taught to forget our native beliefs and to convert to everything white." Many Nez Perce day Washington, northern Idaho, and Montana. This huge landmass was the home of thousands of Native Americans, including the Nez Perce. President Franklin Pierce appointed Isaac Ingalls Stevens the first governor of Washington Territory. In addition, Stevens was to supervise a government survey to determine the course of a railroad route that would run from Minneapolis, Minnesota, to Puget Sound.

The Nez Perce knew little about Governor Stevens. However, they had learned from the Iroquois, the Delaware, and other eastern Indians about the policies of the United States. They had heard about the relocation, or removal, of Indians to reservation lands where white officials called agents controlled all aspects of their life. Rumors spread that whites intended to remove the Indians along the Pacific coast to the interior. According to one Catholic missionary, some Indians believed they would "be banished to the Arctic . . . to a land where the sun never shines." Still, the Nez Perce considered themselves to be strong and independent, capable of dealing with representatives of the federal government.

Governor Stevens was also confident. He had journeyed to the Northwest with a mission. He wanted to make his mark on the region by opening Washington Territory to white settlement and expanding the power of the United States to that part of the Pacific Rim. Stevens believed in Manifest Destiny, the notion that the United

States had a God-given right to expand from shore to shore. He also thought that Indian cultures were inherently inferior to that of white Americans and that Native Americans would benefit from the invasion and rule of people like himself. His attitudes reflected those of many white Americans, particularly American politicians who created Indian policies.

After Stevens arrived in the area of Puget Sound, he and his associates completed a comprehensive report of their railroad survey. This multivolume work was a masterpiece, containing details on Indian life and culture. It also included maps of the region that offered practical transportation routes and indicated the most fertile areas.

In the report, Stevens acknowledged that the Nez Perce and other northwestern Indians had a "natural title" to their homeland. But he also understood that through treaties he could liquidate Indian land titles in the eyes of non-Indians and the government. In this way, he could open the region to white settlement. Stevens did not originate this idea. In fact, it had played a part of the official Indian policy of the United States thoughout the early 19th century. The governor was appointed to execute this policy and hurried to do so. "I confidently expect to accomplish the whole business," Stevens wrote, "extinguishing the Indian title to every acre of land."

When Stevens completed his railroad survey, he ordered his associates,

Isaac Ingalls Stevens, who was appointed governor of Washington Territory in 1853. Stevens believed in Manifest Destiny—the idea that the United States had a God-given right to expand from shore to shore. To aid this goal, he negotiated many treaties that stripped Indian groups of their rights to their homelands.

among them George Gibbs, to make a study of recent Indian treaties. Gibbs and others read agreements made between the United States and the Oto, Omaha, and Missouri tribes. They used these documents to produce the first Indian treaties in the Northwest. Each treaty called for an end to tribal conflicts, sought to establish peace between whites and Indians, and created guidelines for trade between the two groups. More important, the treaties limited Indian lands to small parcels called reservations. They also maintained that the Bureau of Indian Affairs (the federal government's agency in charge of managing Indian affairs) would have supreme power on the reservations. Thus the Indians lost absolute sovereignty over their own affairs and became wards of the government.

Officials intended to use the reservation system to "civilize" the Indians by destroying their traditions and replacing them with American culture. In the words of George Mannypenny, the commissioner of Indian affairs (the head of the BIA), the government could compel reservation Indians to "be domesticated, improved, and elevated" through formal and informal education. In addition, reservations would serve as "fixed, settled, and permanent home[s]" where Indians could learn to be farmers like their white neighbors.

Governor Stevens and other representatives of the United States championed such ideas and made them their objectives. They looked forward to the

Students attending an integrated Catholic school in the early 20th century. Officials and missionaries shared the view that Indians educated in white-run schools would forget their heritage and adopt the ways of non-Indians.

time when Indian elders died, because the officials assumed that the cultural heritage of the people would die with them. Stevens foresaw a day when young Indians would be educated in white schools, where they would learn new ways and forget their own history.

The first treaties Stevens negotiated were with Indians living along the Pacific coast and in the vicinity of Puget Sound. During the proceedings, he did not allow the agreements to be translated into the Indians' languages. Instead, he used Chinook Jargon, a trade dialect, to communicate with the Indians. As a result, the coastal and Puget Sound Indians did not fully understand the treaties, and many refused to sign them. Stevens was little troubled by this. As long as he could get the signatures of a few Indians, he considered a treaty legal. Once signed, Stevens forwarded the treaties to the Senate for ratification and to the president for his signature.

Indians and some whites challenged Stevens's methods. They accused Stevens of rushing the treaty councils and, in the case of the 1854 Treaty of Medicine Creek, of forging Indian signatures. Still, these treaties were all eventually ratified and became law.

After making a whirlwind tour through the Indian territory west of the Cascade Mountains to collect signatures, Stevens sent his agents into eastern Washington to inform the interior Indians of "the objects of the Government in proposing to treat with them, and collecting them at some point favorable for holding Treaties." The messengers explained that Stevens wanted to meet with the Nez Perce, Yakima, Palouse, Cayuse, Walla Walla, Umatilla, and several other tribes in the Walla Walla Valley. This grand council at Walla Walla was to change the lives of all of the Nez Perce. ▲

*A sketch of the Nez Perce leader Red Wolf, drawn by Gustavus So-
hon in 1855. A private in the U.S. Army, Sohon accompanied Governor Stevens to the Walla Walla Council, during which he sketched
the proceedings and made portraits of many of the participants.*

THE
WALLA WALLA
COUNCIL

The Nez Perce learned of the Walla Walla Council from Governor Stevens's assistant, Richard H. Lansdale, and from William Craig. The husband of Chief Big Thunder's daughter, Craig lived among the Nez Perce and spoke their language. He discussed the Americans' Indian policies with the tribe, explaining all about treaties and reservations. Most likely, Craig advised the people to make the best deal possible with the United States because he knew that without a treaty, the tribe might lose all of its land and be removed elsewhere. He also offered to serve as the Nez Perce's advocate, quietly lobbying on their behalf.

On May 24, 1855, the Nez Perce made a grand entry into the council grounds. Approximately 2,500 Indians—men, women, and children—rode on horseback single file into the Walla Walla Valley. They sang as they moved toward a fluttering U.S. flag that had been hoisted by the treaty negotiators. Big Thunder, Old Joseph, Spotted Eagle, Lawyer, Red Wolf, and other chiefs led the procession, which halted about a mile from the flag. In the company of Craig, several of the leaders were then introduced to Stevens and Joel Palmer, the Oregon superintendent of Indian affairs. Following these formalities, approximately "a thousand warriors mounted on fine horses and riding at a gallop, two abreast . . . their faces covered with white, red, and yellow paint in fanciful designs, and decked with plumes and feathers and trinkets fluttering in the sunshine" dashed forward. According to the son of Governor Stevens, who accompanied his father, the Nez Perce exhibited some of their horsemanship, "charging at full gallop . . . [while] firing their guns, brandishing their

Sohon's depiction of the arrival of the Nez Perce at the Walla Walla treaty grounds. According to eyewitness accounts, the Indians, dressed in colorful finery, rode forward at full gallop while yelling, beating drums, and firing guns in the air. The Nez Perce staged their grand entrance to communicate the might of their tribe to the treaty negotiators.

shields, beating their drums, and yelling their war-whoops.'' Some of them dismounted and danced to the drumming and singing. Then they retired to their own encampment to set up their tipis and prepare their meals. Stevens thought that the Indians had put on a grand show on his behalf, and indeed they had. The leaders wanted to impress the governor with their skill, power, and pride. With their dramatic

entrance into the council grounds, they hoped to make the point that the Nez Perce tribe was a great nation.

Stevens and Palmer came to the council with their own goals. They wanted to negotiate two treaties that would create two reservations, onto which many tribes would be relocated. Before the council began, Stevens confidently concluded that ''there is scarcely a doubt that the negotiations will be successful.'' However, when he wrote this statement, he did not know that a delegation of Yakima, Walla Walla, and Cayuse had visited the Nez Perce in the hope of forming a united front to oppose the treaties and reservations. The day before the council opened, some Cayuse leaders visited Utsinmalikin, a Nez Perce chief, and requested that his tribe attend a meeting. ''What are their hearts to us?'' he asked, referring to the Americans. ''Our hearts are Nez Perce hearts,'' he exclaimed, ''and we know them.'' According to this leader, the Nez Perce ''came here to hold a great council with the Great Chief of the Americans, and we know, the straight forward path to pursue and are alone responsible for our actions.''

On May 29, the Indians met the treaty negotiators under brush arbors built for the occasion. The American delegation sat on wooden benches, and the Indians sat on the ground in semicircular rows 40 deep, one behind the other. The first order of business was

Sohon's sketch of the first day of the Walla Walla Council. During the negotiations, the American delegation sat on wooden benches in the middle of the treaty grounds. The Indians surrounded them, seated on the ground in semicircular rows 40 deep.

to swear in the interpreters. Stevens selected William Craig to interpret for the Nez Perce. Although Craig spoke their language, as one Nez Perce pointed out, "he translated literally and often completely misunderstood the sense of the Indian statements." James Doty kept a record of the council for the whites, while Chief Timothy, Chief Lawyer, and a small number of other Nez Perce made their own notes. As James Doty stated, the Indian authors wanted their position "preserved among the archives of the nation and handed down to future generations." Tragically, these notes have been lost, but if they are ever located, they would offer an Indian perspective of the council.

Stevens spoke in a confusing manner, making allusions to Lewis and Clark, William Penn, Andrew Jackson, and Cherokee chief John Ross that had little to do with the matters at hand. Eventually he revealed his major objective:

> What shall we do at this council? We want you and ourselves to agree upon tracts of land where you will live; in those tracts of land we want each man who will work to have his own land, his own horses, his own cattle, and his own home for himself and his children.

Stevens asked the Nez Perce to accept the rule of the Bureau of Indian Affairs. He wanted the men to become reservation ranchers and farmers and "to learn to make ploughs, to learn to make wagons, and everything which you need in your house." To Nez Perce women, he offered the opportunity for instruction in how "to spin, and to weave and to make clothes." Once their parents had mastered these skills, Stevens believed their children could look forward to becoming "farmers and mechanics . . . doctors and lawyers like white men."

The Nez Perce did not find these proposals appealing. The people had little desire to live like whites. They valued their own culture and saw little need to change. However, the Nez Perce understood that the key issue under discussion was land.

To them, the earth was a sacred gift from the Creator. It provided for the people, offering food and water. They likened the land to a mother who nurtures and cares for her children. Thus, selling the earth was like selling one's own mother, and this troubled the Indians.

Some scholars have said that Lawyer and William Craig made a secret deal with Governor Stevens before the council began. By this arrangement, the Nez Perce were to retain their land and their right to fish, hunt, and gather where they always had. In return, the Indians would agree to the governor's treaty and not oppose the government. No documents exist to prove that a prearranged deal was in fact struck, but some Indians maintained that this was the case. Young Chief of the Cayuse and Yellow Bird of the Walla Walla suspected as much. "Now I will speak about Lawyer," said Yellow Bird. "I think my friend has given his land, that is what I think from his words."

Eagle from the Light, Red Grizzly Bear, and Red Wolf were among the Nez Perce leaders who spoke at the council. But Lawyer's words seemed to have been given the most attention. Some Nez Perce today maintain that the government was dishonest in their dealings, because Stevens treated Lawyer as the head chief of the Nez Perce, a position that did not exist in the tribe's world. Perhaps Lawyer was simply a camp crier (someone who transmitted news from one village to another), but his position at the council was rarely challenged by other Nez Perce chiefs. Even when Old Looking Glass, a man of great stature of the buffalo-hunting and warrior class, arrived late to the council, he did not challenge the direction of the proceedings. Because the Nez Perce Treaty would recognize the right of the people to their traditional homelands, the chiefs followed Lawyer's lead.

Early in the council, Lawyer said that he trusted Stevens and Palmer. He argued that the president had sent the agents to the Nez Perce "to take care of . . . white people and . . . red people." He called American Indian policy the "new law" and told the council, "Our old laws are poor, the new laws we are getting are good laws, are straight." He said to the Americans, "I shall do you no wrong, and you do me none, both our rights shall be protected forever; it is not for ourselves here that we are

Lawyer's role in the Walla Walla proceedings created discord among the Nez Perce chiefs. Although many followed Lawyer's lead and signed the treaty that Stevens presented them, some accused him of having made a secret deal with the governor before the council began.

talking, it is for those that come that we are speaking."

Later in the council, Lawyer set forth his position more boldly: "From the time of Columbus and from the time of Lewis and Clark we have known our friends . . . known you as brothers." Because Stevens had been "sent by the President to take care of his children," Lawyer agreed to accept the help. The governor replied that he had "the heart

IMPORTANT LOCATIONS IN EARLY-19TH-CENTURY NEZ PERCE HISTORY

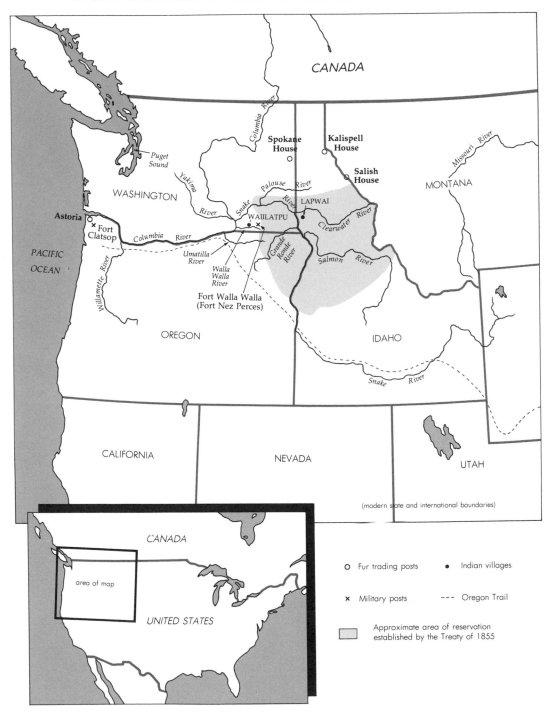

CANADA

Puget
Sound

WASHINGTON

Spokane
House

Kalispell
House

Salish
House

MONTANA

Columbia River

Yakima River

Astoria

Fort
Clatsop

PACIFIC
OCEAN

Columbia River

Palouse River

Snake River

WAIILATPU

LAPWAI

Clearwater River

Missouri River

Umatilla
River

Walla
Walla
River

Fort Walla Walla
(Fort Nez Perces)

Grande
Ronde
River

Salmon River

Willamette River

OREGON

IDAHO

CALIFORNIA

NEVADA

Snake River

UTAH

(modern state and international boundaries)

CANADA

area of map

UNITED STATES

○ Fur trading posts   ● Indian villages

✕ Military posts   - - - Oregon Trail

         Approximate area of reservation
         established by the Treaty of 1855

of the Nes Perses through their Chief" and that "our hearts are one." Palmer also proclaimed that the "heart of the Nes Perses and ours are one."

Old Looking Glass, Big Thunder, Old Joseph, Eagle from the Light, Red Grizzly Bear, and other Nez Perce chiefs listened and agreed with Lawyer. Their hearts were one with the Americans at Walla Walla, but this was not so with the Palouse, Yakima, Umatilla, Cayuse, Walla Walla, and Columbia River tribes. Some of them opposed the treaties they were offered. In the end, they felt they had no choice but to agree to them. It became clear that they could either sign these treaties and secure some land or refuse and retain nothing. Few Indians left the council happy. According to Benjamin Franklin Shaw, one of the governor's aides, the Indians were angry that Stevens had "crammed" the treaties "down their throats in a hurry."

Because of the opposition of the Umatilla, Cayuse, and Walla Walla, the agents decided to negotiate a third treaty, creating another reservation. By June 11, 1855, they had succeeded. The three treaties established the Nez Perce, Yakima, and Umatilla reservations. During the council, Stevens assured the Indians that the treaties would not go into effect for two or three years. Thus, the Indians did not have to adhere to the articles of the treaties or move onto the reservations until the Senate and president had signed the documents. (This did not occur until 1859.)

Governor Stevens also gave his solemn oath that whites would not settle the region until the treaties became law. However, immediately after the signings, he wrote dispatches to major newspapers announcing the opening of the inland Northwest. On June 23, 1855, the *Oregon Weekly Times* ran an article stating that "the country embraced in these cessions and not included in the reservation is open to settlement." Gold, not farms and ranches, brought the first large influx of whites into the region. After miners discovered gold north of the Spokane River near Fort Colvile, a rush began that led to a major Indian war on the Columbia Plateau.

For the most part, the Nez Perce did not participate in the Plateau Indian War of 1855-58. During the early part of the conflict, most of the fighting occurred along the Columbia and Yakima rivers in central Washington Territory. But when the regular army could not locate the hostile Indians in Yakima territory, volunteer soldiers turned their attentions south of the Snake River. One colonel, James K. Kelly, pushed the peaceful Walla Walla into war by murdering Yellow Bird, who had surrendered to the troops under a flag of truce. Colonel Thomas Cornelius stirred up the Cayuse, Palouse, and Umatilla by invading their lands and killing a few people. Colonel Benjamin Franklin Shaw and his Washington Volunteers also made an unprovoked attack on an Indian village situated along the rugged banks of the Grande Ronde River of northeastern Oregon. In the attack, the soldiers killed at least 27 men, women, and children from the Palouse, Cayuse, and Walla Walla tribes.

During the attack on the Grande Ronde, a Nez Perce scout named Captain John served with Shaw. His participation was not typical of most Nez Perce. The majority of Nez Perce chose not to become involved in the war, and most of those who did were young men.

On April 12, 1858, about 15 Indian warriors stole the cattle herd grazing close to Fort Walla Walla. (This was not the old Hudson's Bay post but a military fort established farther east near present-day Walla Walla, Washington.) Soon afterward, a band of hostile Indians killed two French miners crossing the Columbia Plateau north of the Snake River. Colonel Edward Steptoe, commander of Fort Walla Walla, believed that a band of Palouse Indians had stolen the herd and killed the miners. Thus, he decided the tribe should be punished. On May 6, Colonel Steptoe led a force of nearly 160 men northeast to find and destroy the Palouse warriors. He also intended to travel as far north as Colville, Washington, the site of the recent gold discovery. With his military force, he planned to calm the Indians there, who were upset about the invasion and destruction of their land by white miners.

En route to the land of the Palouse Indians, Steptoe and his men traveled through Nez Perce country. At the Snake River, he met Chief Timothy. The Nez Perce leader and some other Indians operated a ferry business across the river at its junction with Alpowa Creek. Timothy agreed to transport Steptoe and his horses, cannons, baggage, and goods to the north side of the river. When the Indians completed this job, the chief, his brother Levi, and 13 other Nez Perces offered to scout for Steptoe.

At the time, Timothy was engaged in a bitter dispute with Chief Tilcoax of the Palouse. The two Indian leaders hated each other for several reasons, a few of which are known. Timothy was a pro-white, pro-Christian, and pro-treaty Indian who knew how to read and write English. At the Walla Walla Council he had supported the Nez Perce Treaty and signed it. Tilcoax considered himself a "traditional" Indian, not a "progressive" like Timothy. Tilcoax was antiwhite, anti-Christian, and antitreaty. But he had participated in the Walla Walla Council and had reportedly signed the Yakima Treaty. A short time after the council ended, Tilcoax joined the war party, refusing to abide by the agreements signed in the summer of 1855.

When Steptoe arrived at Timothy's village, the two Indian leaders were engaged in a feud. Timothy knew that a large number of Palouse and other Indians had organized north of the river and intended to stop Steptoe's advance. Some of Timothy's people had warned Steptoe of their presence, but

continued on page 57

PLATEAU FINERY

In the early 19th century, the first non-Indian traders who came in contact with the Nez Perce introduced them to many new goods. Among those most welcomed by the tribe were glass beads and woolen cloth. The Nez Perce soon began to use these manufactured products to make and decorate their horse gear, ceremonial objects, and clothing.

Although the goods were non-Indian in origin, the Nez Perce looked to other Indian artists for inspiration in how to use them. During buffalo-hunting expeditions on the Plains, they saw the geometric beadwork patterns favored by tribes such as the Cheyenne and soon began to copy these designs. Another great influence was the beautiful horse gear of the Crow Indians. Crow traders often visited the Nez Perce, offering to exchange their tribe's beaded handiwork for the Nez Perce's horses. Eventually, the Nez Perce learned to produce the same designs they so admired on Crow-made objects.

Eastern Indians employed as servants and boatmen by Canadian traders acquainted the Nez Perce with still more design possibilities. The Indians of the Northeast and Great Lakes had long created beaded floral patterns in imitation of designs they saw on European woven cloth. The Nez Perce followed their example, but developed their own innovations, most notably in their choice of colors. Eastern Indians often preferred dark shades, whereas the Nez Perce loved vivid reds, pinks, blues, and purples. The fineries made by the Nez Perce are among the most brightly colored objects created by all Indian groups.

Beaded ornaments such as this were worn on the foreheads of the Nez Perce's horses during special social and ceremonial occasions.

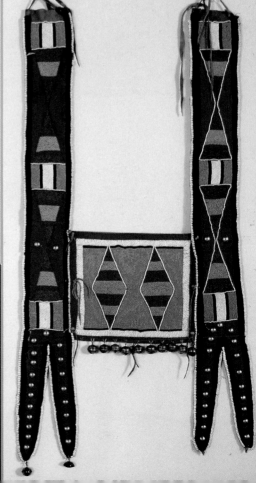

A martingale, or horse collar, made from red woolen cloth and adorned with glass beads, brass bells, and dyed horsehair tassels.

The outlining of shapes and the use of isosceles triangles in the pattern on this martingale are characteristic of the work of Crow artists.

A woman's saddle carved from green cottonwood. Excellent examples of Nez Perce beadwork are found on the pommels and stirrup.

The red cloth of this martingale came from a Hudson's Bay Company blanket. Other materials used include brass sequins, purple and blue felt, and blue and red beads.

*A headdress constructed from wool cloth and rawhide,
decorated with glass beads, and topped with deer antlers.
It was worn by a medicine man during ceremonies and*

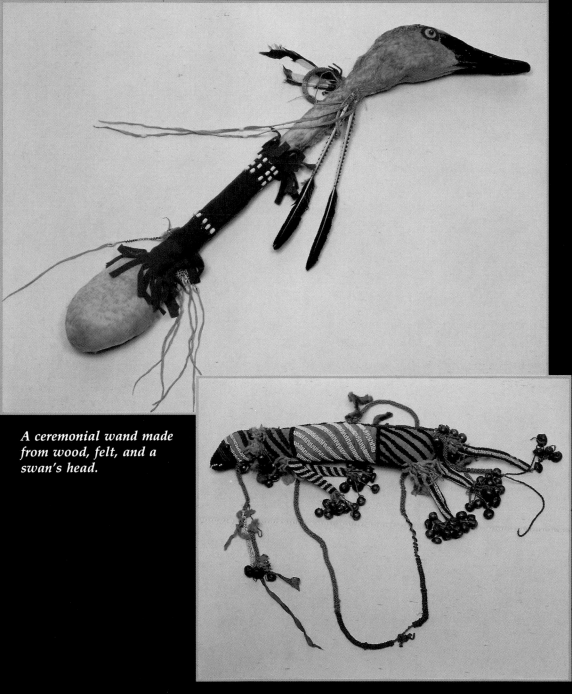

A ceremonial wand made from wood, felt, and a swan's head.

A beaded otter effigy that was used in healing ceremonies. Brass bells are attached to its neck, feet, and tail.

A pair of leather gloves adorned with fringe. The intricate floral patterns show the influence of Great Lakes Indian beadwork on Nez Perce artisans.

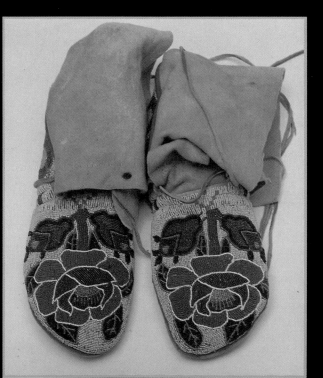

A single red flower decorates the toe of each of these beaded moccasins.

The red, white, and blue beads on this pair of moccasins create a geometric design reminiscent of those used by Indian artists of the Plains.

The glass beads on this early-19th-century elk hide dress were made in Italy, China, and the Netherlands, evidence of the wealth of foreign goods then available to the Nez Perce through their dealings with non-Indian traders.

continued from page 48

the colonel ignored them. As long as Steptoe was committed to heading forward, Timothy decided that, acting as a scout, he could use the soldiers to get to his enemy.

The Nez Perce scouts led the soldiers north through a steep ravine, leading out of a deep canyon and onto the wide green hill country of the plateau above. The group then moved along the present-day border of Washington and Idaho. On May 15, Steptoe wrote that "the Palouse are in front of us—we expect to come up to them today." He believed his men would give the Indians "a good drubbing," but the colonel had not prepared his soldiers for the fight that awaited them. Before leaving Fort Walla Walla, Steptoe had outfitted his men with only 40 rounds of ammunition and had ordered them to leave their sabers behind. More than half of his men were inadequately armed, with short, widemouthed musketoons that were accurate for only about 50 yards. Clearly, Steptoe did not expect to fight a pitched battle.

That day, more than 1,000 warriors joined forces to block Steptoe's advance. The Indians had sung, prayed, and met in council to prepare for battle, and now they were ready for war. One soldier wrote that the Indians were an "awesome sight to the inexperienced command." Steptoe had expected a small band of Palouse warriors and instead found himself in the center of "ten or twelve hundred Indians of various tribes—Spokanes, Palouses,

The progressive Nez Perce leader Timothy acted as a scout for Colonel Edward Steptoe, the commander of Fort Walla Walla. Embroiled in a bitter feud with a Palouse chief, Timothy told Steptoe he could locate the band of Palouse whom the colonel believed was responsible for the murder of two white miners.

Coeur d'Alenes, Yakimas, and some others—all armed, painted, and defiant." The Indians followed Steptoe to a small lake, where the soldiers were resting. The Indians did not attack but sat on their colorfully painted horses watching the soldiers. Several Indian delegations visited Steptoe, including one led by Chief Vincent, a Coeur d'Alene.

Vincent talked to Steptoe through his interpreter, Father Joseph Joset. The Indians wanted to know why Steptoe had brought along so many troops and cannons. While Steptoe talked to Vincent and Joset, the Nez Perce scouts grew impatient. Timothy's brother Levi advanced toward Vincent and Steptoe. Taking out his riding whip, Levi struck Vincent either on the face or shoulder and said, "Proud man, why do you not fire?" The incident caused a commotion. Levi then turned to another Coeur d'Alene Indian and accused him of wanting to fire on the soldiers. Vincent angrily responded to Levi that "hereafter you will be ashamed of having struck" another Indian. Vincent rode off.

In the meantime, some of the young men in the Indian force began fighting among themselves. Their elders cautioned them to stop quarreling and remember that their true enemies were

The Steptoe Battle of 1858, drawn by Sohon several months after the fight took place. Expecting to engage a small group of Palouse, Steptoe was surprised by an attack of more than 1,000 warriors from various tribes. After a full day of battle, Steptoe's men made a hasty retreat, barely escaping with their life.

the soldiers. Eager for battle, a few of the warriors, mostly Coeur d'Alene Indians, then rode pell-mell toward the soldiers, firing guns at them. The soldiers took the fire until the youngsters were directly in front of them. Steptoe ordered his men to fire, and they immediately killed three of the Indians—James Nehlukteltshiye, Victor Smena, and Zachary Natatkem. When the smoke cleared and the warriors saw the three dead, many of the other warriors raced at breakneck speed to engage the soldiers.

In the running battle, more than 1,000 angry Indians chased the soldiers to Pine Creek. On a sloping hill above the creek, Steptoe made his last stand. He fought all day and into the evening. Steptoe, Timothy, and the others then found themselves with few bullets, no water, and in grave danger. The colonel considered a fight to the finish in hand-to-hand combat. But his men did not support the idea, so Steptoe determined "to run the gauntlet, so that if possible some might escape." The soldiers buried their howitzers and slipped off the hill.

Some accounts say that the Nez Perce scouts led the soldiers through the Indian lines undetected. This is highly unlikely given the fact that more than 150 men, including the wounded, rode horseback off the hill. They made sufficient noise to be heard. Even if they had slipped through the lines, the Indians could have easily outraced the scouts and soldiers to the Snake River. The Palouse, Coeur d'Alene, Spokane, and others had fresh horses; the Nez Perce did not. It is more likely that the Indians allowed the scouts and soldiers to retreat. This was the nature of Plateau Indian warfare. The Indians had killed, wounded, and embarrassed their enemy, so they felt they could afford to be generous.

Despite Steptoe's defeat, the fighting did not end. Without the support of the Nez Perce scouts, Colonel George Wright led an army onto the Northwest Plateau in the fall of 1858. Wright engaged the Indians in the battles of Four Lakes and Spokane Plain. He pushed them from the field, kidnapped women and children as hostages, and hanged more than 15 warriors.

Wright's campaign ended the Plateau Indian War, a conflict in which the Nez Perce had barely participated. Most Nez Perce chose neutrality over hostility, but their lands and sovereignty had not been threatened directly. Soon, however, non-Indians would bring trouble to Nez Perce country. This time, the result would be a full-scale Nez Perce war. ▲

Chief Joseph, the Nez Perce leader who eloquently protested the reduction of the Nez Perce reservation in 1863. Included in the territory seized was the home of Joseph's band—the Wallowa Valley in northeastern Oregon. Joseph claimed he loved "that beautiful valley of winding waters . . . more than all the rest of the world."

THE
GATHERING
STORM

Gold—the mineral that was so greatly desired by the Americans—was a misfortune to the Indians. The discovery of gold near Colville, Washington, had drawn miners into the Northwest and triggered the Plateau Indian War. Prospecting in the Bitterroot Mountains in Nez Perce territory would also spark conflict.

As early as 1852, a prospector named Elias D. Pierce claimed to have discovered gold in the Bitterroots. In 1858, he and his partner, Seth Ferrell, found the mineral on the Clearwater River in the heart of Nez Perce country, and 2 years later, Pierce and 10 other miners struck gold on Canal Gulch, a tributary of the Clearwater River. The Nez Perce Treaty prohibited non-Indians from mining on the reservation. Thus, Pierce and the others lied, saying that they had found gold east of the reservation.

At first, the Nez Perce agent, A. J. Cain, was able to keep most miners off the Indians' lands. But as word of the gold strike circulated, miners rushed onto the reservation, totally ignoring the agent, the treaty, and the Nez Perce people who protested the violation.

The miners built tent cities at Lewiston, Florence, and Elk City, which drew gamblers, prostitutes, whiskey peddlers, and merchants to Nez Perce land. These characters, often romanticized in books and films about the American West, were a rough bunch who disliked the Indians and disregarded their legal rights.

Whites throughout the Northwest began to pressure the government to negotiate a new treaty with the Nez Perce in order to reestablish the reservation boundaries so that the area where gold had been discovered would be outside of Nez Perce territory. In May 1862, the Senate appropriated money to renegotiate a smaller reservation. In July, government officials Calvin H. Hale, Charles Hutchinson, and S. D. Howe traveled to Fort Lapwai to discuss a new treaty.

The officials did not meet with the Nez Perce until May 1863, when they held a major council at Fort Lapwai. The Lapwai Council opened on May 25, before the arrival of several important chiefs, including Old Joseph, White Bird, and Eagle from the Light. Hale convened the people to tell them that the purpose of the meeting was to invalidate the Nez Perce Treaty of 1855 and create the Nez Perce Treaty of 1863. The result, he candidly informed his au-

dience, would be a smaller reservation. All of the chiefs in attendance said that they would not sell their lands. Even Chief Lawyer, the old friend of the whites, told Hale that they would not agree to the redrawing of the reservation's borders.

Hale then tried to convince the Indians that the United States's proposal to reduce the size of the reservation was for the good of the Nez Perce. He argued that the army could better protect the people and that the miners would be off the reservation. But Lawyer and

In the 1850s, gold was discovered in the Bitterroot Mountains in what is now eastern Idaho. As prospectors flocked to the area, the mineral was also found on the Nez Perce Indian Reservation. The Nez Perce Treaty of 1855 prohibited non-Indians from mining on reservation land, but most fortune-seeking prospectors simply ignored the provision.

the others stood firm. Lawyer even took out a notebook and read aloud the words of Governor Stevens: "My friends, we have assembled under the influence of Laws, and that which shall be permanent and straight." The chief made his point well, so well that Hale adjourned the meeting.

The next day, Lawyer told Hale that "we cannot give you the country you ask for" and maintained that the Nez Perce Treaty of 1855 was "permanent, sacred, and according to law." He further explained:

> With pleasure we have listened to the words brought from the President from time to time. Hence the reason I asked you the other day, whether propositions so unlike the other, came from him. I say to you, you trifle with us. The boundary was fixed, and we have been under it and thought it permanent. We understood that the whole of our reservation was for us, to cultivate and to occupy as we pleased. . . . You but trifle with us. We cannot give you the country, we cannot sell it to you.

Other Nez Perce leaders felt that Hale's proposition "did not look good, it looks crooked." The Indians did not waver from this position, and the council did not meet in session for six days. When it finally reopened, Old Joseph, Eagle from the Light, Big Thunder, White Bird, and other chiefs had arrived. After a meeting with Hale, the leaders talked among themselves. They then told Hale that they would sell some land around the gold mines and an area near the new town of Lewiston in Idaho Territory. However, this offer was not good enough for Hale, so he changed his tactics. He decided to try meeting with the chiefs in private conferences.

The commissioners met with the Indian leaders one by one, trying to convince them to surrender their land. Many still did not waver in their refusal to renegotiate the treaty. However, Lawyer argued that if the new reservation was sufficiently large, he would agree to it. Timothy of Alpowa and Jason of Asotin agreed as well, provided they could continue to live off the reservation. The Nez Perce who opposed the negotiations were outraged. They maintained that the commissioners had no authority to destroy the Nez Perce Treaty of 1855 without the consent of all of the tribe's leaders.

Ignoring this faction, representatives of the federal government concluded a new treaty with Lawyer and 51 Nez Perce men who were not chiefs. Ultimately, the Nez Perce Treaty of 1863 cut the reservation to one-tenth its original size. It ceded to the government 6,932,270 acres, for which the tribe was given less than 8 cents an acre in compensation.

The antitreaty faction felt that the Thief Treaty, as they called it, was illegal. It insisted that Lawyer and his friends could not sell lands that did not belong to them. Years later, Young Joseph—a Nez Perce chief known to his people as Hinmahtooyahlatkekht

Nez Perce chiefs Timothy, Lawyer, and Jason (seated, left to right) and four unidentified white men in an 1868 photograph probably taken in New York City after the chiefs had negotiated an amendment to the controversial 1863 treaty with officials in Washington, D.C.

(Thunder Rising over Loftier Mountain Heights)—reflected upon this treaty, saying that if the antitreaty Indians "ever owned the land, we own it still, for we never sold it."

In the early 1870s, Nez Perce agent John Monteith and Oregon superintendent of Indian affairs T. B. Ordeneal came to agree with Joseph's view. After conducting an investigation, the two men wrote H. R. Clum, the commissioner of Indian affairs:

> If any respect is to be paid to the laws and customs of the Indians then the treaty of 1863 is not binding upon Joseph and his band. If so, then Wallowa Valley [in northeastern Oregon] is still part of the Nez Perce reservation; this being the case, then the Government is equitably bound to pay the white settlers for their improvements and for the trouble, inconvenience and expense of removing from there.

The commissioner agreed with his agents and asked his superior, the secretary of the interior, to set aside the Wallowa Valley "for the exclusive use of said Indians and that white settlers be advised that they are prohibited from entering or settling in said valley." On June 16, 1873, President Ulysses S. Grant signed an executive order that granted lands in the valley to the Nez Perce. Unfortunately, the boundaries for this new reservation were misguided. The Indians most wanted the government to recognize their claims to Wallowa Lake and the upper part of Wallowa River. Instead, the order gave the Nez Perce the valley's lower meadows, which had largely been settled by whites.

Ordeneal and Monteith had not made the mistake. It was the error of some official in Washington, D.C., but the superintendent and the agent were unable to correct it. Instead of resolving a decade-old problem, the executive order only made matters worse. Indians and whites were unsatisfied and alarmed as fear and rumors of conflict swept across the prairie. Oregon governor Lafayette F. Grover and Oregon's congressional delegation sided with the settlers who wanted Joseph and his followers removed to the Nez Perce reservation in Idaho. They lied to the president, Congress, and the secretary of the interior, stating that "Joseph's band do not desire Wallowa Valley for a reservation and a home."

Young Joseph had spent his life worrying that one day the whites would take his land. Now it appeared to him and others that that day was at hand. However, the chief would not relinquish his land without first trying to

do everything in his power to prevent it. In August 1871, Joseph's father—Old Joseph—died at his village in the Wallowa Valley. Before his death, Old Joseph reminded his children of the sacredness of the earth on which they lived. Nearly eight years later, Young Joseph shared his father's words in an interview he gave to the *North American Review*.

> My body is returning to my mother earth, and my spirit is going very soon to see the Great Spirit Chief. When I am gone, think of your country. You are the chief of these people. They look to you to guide them. Always remember that your father never sold his country. You must stop your ears whenever you are asked to sign a treaty selling your home. A few years more, and white men will be all around you. They have their eyes on this land. My son, never forget my dying words. This country holds your father's body. Never sell the bones of your father and mother.

Joseph buried his father "in that beautiful valley of winding waters." He admitted that he loved "that land more than all the rest of the world. A man who would not love his father's grave is worse than a wild animal." But no amount of love of the earth could help Joseph with the immense problems he was facing.

Many forces were working against him. An 1873 rebellion of the Modoc Indians of Oregon had convinced even more white politicians that all Indians should be placed on reservations. Whites were also becoming worried about the growing influence of Native American holy people, especially prophets among the northwestern Indians who taught that their people should reject Christianity, white rule, reservations, and removal. Spiritual leaders often opposed Christianity because they felt its introduction would split their communities. Perhaps Chief Joseph said it best when he once told some whites that he did not want Christian churches among his people. "They will teach us to quarrel about God," he explained.

Joseph, White Bird, Toohoolhoolzote, Red Heart, and other Nez Perce believed in an old Indian faith, the Washani. Agent Monteith disliked and distrusted this faith and its leadership. Although he had originally championed Joseph's claim of the Wallowa Valley, he changed his mind and told the chief that all the Nez Perce would have to move onto the reservation where they could be watched and controlled. Thus, Joseph lost one of his greatest supporters just when he

Indian agent John B. Monteith (standing) and three Christian Nez Perces who had been educated at the Spalding Mission. In the early 1870s, Monteith urged the commissioner of Indian affairs to restore the Wallowa Valley to the Nez Perce.

needed him most.

Settlers' pressure on the federal government to take back the Wallowa Valley increased. Bowing to their demands, the Bureau of Indian Affairs refused to recognize Grant's executive order and advanced a proposal to remove all the non-Christian, nonreservation, nontreaty Nez Perce onto the reservation. Acting on the advice of others, the president then rescinded his own order on June 10, 1875.

During these developments, General Oliver O. Howard became the commander of the Department of the Columbia. Stationed at Fort Vancouver in what is now southwestern Washington State, Howard made a quick study of the region. He learned about the Nez Perce's situation and agreed with other military men that the whole affair could lead to war. In the spring of 1875, Joseph met Howard while the two men were visiting the Umatilla reservation in present-day Oregon. After speaking with the chief and making his own investigation, Howard wrote: "I think it a great mistake to take from Joseph and his band of Nez Perces Indians that valley. The white people really do not want it." Most of the white settlers in the Wallowa Valley in fact were willing to move out as long as the government compensated them for their land and improvements. Yet their views, like those of General Howard and Chief Joseph, were ignored.

Howard and other whites also came to believe that the Nez Perce Treaty of 1863 was in fact a Thief Treaty. Neither Joseph nor his father had surrendered their home, and the government had no legal claim to the Wallowa Valley. Howard felt so strongly about the matter that he sent Major Henry Clay Wood to stage another investigation. Wood studied the situation in the valley and submitted his findings to the general in a report titled "Joseph and His Land Claims, or Status of Young Joseph and His Band of Nez Perce Indians." His entire report is revealing, particularly his conclusion.

> The non-treaty Nez Perces cannot in law be regarded as bound by the treaty of 1863; and in so far as it attempts to deprive them of a right to occupancy of any land, its provisions are null and void. The extinguishment of their title of occupancy contemplated by this treaty is imperfect and incomplete.

Armed with Wood's report and the support of many people—Indians and non-Indians—Howard traveled to Washington, D.C., in 1876. He wanted to convince the government not to take the valley from Joseph and his band of Nez Perce Indians. He wanted another commission to meet with the Nez Perce to discuss the final disposition of the Wallowa. Like Joseph, the general wished that a new council would result in the restoration of a reservation in the Indians' homeland. He had no way of knowing that the treaty negotiations he was about to set in motion would mark the beginning of the end for any such hope. ▲

Walla-qua-mit, Chu-ya, and Jim White (left to right), photographed on the Colville Indian Reservation, circa 1900. White was a younger brother of White Bird's, one of the Nez Perce leaders who most strongly resisted signing treaties that would cede tribal land to the United States.

GOOD-BYE
TO THE
HOMELAND

The secretary of the interior selected five men to serve as commissioners to deal with the Nez Perce: David H. Jerome, A. C. Barstow, William Stickney, Major Wood, and General Howard. The commissioners arrived at Lapwai, the headquarters of the Nez Perce Agency, on November 7, 1876. The instructions they had been given were clear: "Lose no time in sending for the non-treaty Nez Perce Indians, and especially for Joseph."

The government's eagerness to negotiate was in large part due to events that had taken place on the Great Plains far to the east of Nez Perce territory. In June 1876, Sioux, Cheyenne, and Arapaho warriors had won a momentous victory against the army at the Battle of Little Bighorn in present-day Montana. In 1876, the Indians killed Colonel George Armstrong Custer and more than 200 of his men. Victory celebra-

tions were short-lived, as the army pursued Crazy Horse, Gall, Sitting Bull, and other leaders responsible for the attack. The death of Custer and his troopers caused a public outcry from the settlers to corral all nonreservation Indians. The Nez Perce were to feel the sting of this backlash.

By November 13, Joseph and his band had arrived, and the Lapwai Council began. The commissioners immediately asked Joseph to move his people from the Wallowa Valley to the Nez Perce reservation. As the request involved the earth and as the earth was a spiritual matter, the leader responded with reference to his religion. "The Creative Power," Joseph began, "when he made the earth, made no marks, no lines of division or separation on it." Joseph said that "the earth was [his] mother" and that he "was made of the earth and grew up on its bosom." He also explained that the Nez Perce believed that the land was "too sacred to be valued by or sold for silver or gold."

Although Howard had supported Joseph's claim to the Wallowa Valley, he did not respect the spiritual beliefs of the nontreaty Nez Perce. After Lawyer signed the Thief Treaty, Old Joseph had torn apart his copy of the New Testament. His family made a break with Christianity and instead gravitated to the traditional beliefs of their people. Howard, who was nicknamed the Christian General, called the Washani faith a "new-fangled religious delusion" and labeled the spiritual leaders "wizards" and "magicians." The general believed that the Indian medicine people were more akin to the devil and witches than anything holy. Besides, he felt they fomented discord among the Indians.

When Joseph told Howard that the Indians would not give up the Wallowa Valley at the council, the general became angry. He accused "Indian Joseph and his malcontents" of "[denying] the jurisdiction of the United States over them." Joseph would have agreed with this assessment. He responded with "We will not sell the land. We will not give up the land. We love the land; it is our home."

Years later, Joseph explained his position and that of the nontreaty Nez Perce with a parable:

> Suppose a white man should come to me and say, "Joseph, I like your horses, and I want to buy them."

Joseph would respond, "my horses suit me, I will not sell them." When Joseph responded that he was uninterested in selling his horses, the white man goes to my neighbor, and says to him: "Joseph has some good horses. I want to buy them, but he refuses to sell." My neighbor answers, "Pay me the money, and I will sell you Joseph's horses." The white man returns to me and says, "Joseph, I have bought your horses, and you must let me have them." If we sold our lands to the Government, this is the way they were bought.

The Lapwai Council of 1876 ended with the Nez Perce's refusal to concede to the government. The commissioners left Lapwai disappointed that the Indians "firmly declined" to surrender their lands. Howard and his associates blamed their failure on the *tooats*, the medicine people, who opposed the sale of land and the authority of the United States. His view of the tooats was presented in the annual report to the commissioner of Indian affairs in 1876.

The dreamers among other pernicious doctrines, teach that the earth being created by God complete, should not be disturbed by man, and that any cultivation of the soil or other

Two Moons (far right), the principal tooat *(medicine person) at Nespelem, performing a dance for an audience of Nez Perce and non-Indians. Because the tooats believed that the earth belonged to God and should not be disturbed by humans, they used their influence among their people to block the sale of Nez Perce land to whites.*

improvements to interfere with its natural productions, any voluntary submission to the control of the government, an improvement in the way of schools, churches, etc., are crimes from which they shrink.

Howard and Monteith wanted the Washani leaders to "be required to return to the agencies . . . and in case of refusal that they be removed from further contact with the roaming Indians by immediate transportation to the Indian Territory [present-day Oklahoma]." The commissioners felt that the army should occupy the Wallowa Valley and that all the nontreaty Indians—including people of both the Nez Perce and Upper Palouse tribes—be forced to move to the Nez Perce reservation. The Palouse Indians had been drawn into the controversy by American settlers who wanted their removal from the "public domain" along the Snake River. In January 1877, Monteith asked Howard to bring his troops to the valley. The agent wanted the nontreaty Indians on the reservation by April 1. Howard felt his requests were unreasonable. The appearance of troops in the Wallowa Valley could push the Indians into war, and the general had no interest in triggering an armed conflict.

Joseph argued that the territory claimed by the Americans "belonged to my father, and when he died it was given to me and my people, and I will not leave it until I am compelled to." The nontreaty Nez Perce and Palouse concurred with Joseph, but they were

In his negotiations with the nontreaty Nez Perce at the Second Lapwai Council, General Oliver Otis Howard displayed little patience for the Indians' religious beliefs about their homeland. He eventually lost his temper with Toohoolhoolzote, a tooat who had been chosen to speak for the Indians and who refused to be placed on a reservation.

alarmed by rumors about the troops. Ollokot, Joseph's younger brother, asked Howard and Monteith for another meeting to negotiate a resolution. On May 3, 1877, the nontreaty Indians—the Nez Perce and the Palouse—

came together with Howard and Monteith for the second Lapwai Council.

Before the meeting, the nontreaty Indians held their own council. They selected Toohoolhoolzote to speak with Howard in their behalf. After the Palouse bands arrived, the Indians also asked Husishusis Kute to speak for them. Both men were respected religious leaders who understood the relationship of the people with the land. As a young man, Toohoolhoolzote had gained fame as a powerful hunter and warrior. By the 1860s, he had become a medicine man and leader of a band living along the Snake River just south of the mouth of the Salmon River. Husishusis Kute led a band of Palouse living at Wawawai, a village downstream several miles from Toohoolhoolzote's home. Also a warrior in his youth, Husishusis Kute was known as one of the "new religious people" who used "a drum to beat in his worship." The others did not use drums in the religious service until Husishusis Kute did. General Howard disliked Husishusis Kute and described him as "the oily, wily, bright-eyed young chief."

Husishusis Kute never had an opportunity to express his views at the council because of an ugly quarrel that developed between Toohoolhoolzote and Howard. The trouble started when Ollokot began to argue with the general. He told Howard that whereas Indians respected whites, the settlers treated Indians like dogs. "I sometimes think my friends are different from what I had supposed," he said. In order

for Indians and whites to live together, Ollokot proposed that "there should be one law for all." The "law" was a major theme at the council, and Toohoolhoolzote continued with the subject. His message to Howard was that the Nez Perce had always believed in the Law but that their Law came from the Creator. The white man's law did not come from this higher source and thus lacked the divine substance of Indian Law. Toohoolhoolzote spoke of the "chieftainship of the earth," which was part of the supreme Indian Law. Such talk angered the Christian General, who expressed his dislike for the Indian tooat.

Howard would later describe Toohoolhoolzote as "broad-shouldered, deep-chested, thick-necked, five feet ten in height, had a heavy guttural voice, and betrayed in every word a strong and settled hatred of all Caucasians." Howard called Toohoolhoolzote the "cross-grained growler," a man who was an "ugly, obstinate savage of the worst type." With the passing of time, Toohoolhoolzote became "crosser and more impudent in his abruptness of manner." The Nez Perce leader did not like Howard or the policies of his government. He did not mask his contempt for Howard, but he carefully kept a cool head, forcefully setting forth the position of the nontreaty Indians.

Toohoolhoolzote told Howard that he had "heard of a bargain, a trade between some of these Indians and the white men concerning their land." This was a reference to Lawyer and the Nez

Perce who had signed the Thief Treaty of 1863. Some of the Indians had sold their lands, Toohoolhoolzote asserted, but he had not. "I belong to the land out of which I came," he stated. Howard responded by falsely stating that a "majority" of the Nez Perce had signed the treaty ceding the land to the United States. The general maintained that "the non-treaty Indians being in the minority in their opposition, were bound by that agreement, and must abide by it." The nontreaty people disagreed with this line of reasoning. No person could force them to follow a treaty that they did not sign.

In every session of the 1877 Lapwai Council, Toohoolhoolzote pointed this out. The land, Toohoolhoolzote said, "should not be disturbed by hoe or plough," and "man should subsist on what grows of itself." The tooat was worried that the Indians would be separated from lands that belonged to them "by inheritance." He repeated his ideas concerning "chieftainship" of the earth. "Chieftainship cannot be sold, cannot be given away," he said. Howard responded that the United States did "not wish to interfere with your religion." In truth, the government had long sought to Christianize and "civilize" the Indians. Howard's desire to move the Indians from their traditional land was an act against Indian Law and their deepest spiritual beliefs.

The more Toohoolhoolzote spoke, the more Howard became angry. He became so irritated that he raised his voice, saying: "Twenty times over you repeat that the earth is your mother, and about the chieftainship of the earth. Let us hear it no more, but come to business at once." To the Nez Perce and the Palouse, the business at hand was the sacredness of the earth—their "mother." To Howard, the business was American Indian policy, especially the removal of the nontreaty people onto a reservation, where the Bureau of Indian Affairs could rule their lives.

Toohoolhoolzote responded to Howard, saying, "You white people get together, measure the earth, and then divided it; so I want you to talk directly what you mean!" Again Howard explained that the treaty the Nez Perce had signed in 1863 required all Indians to move to the reservation. This law, Howard said, came from Washington, D.C., and he had to enforce the law. "Part of the Indians gave up their land," Toohoolhoolzote said. "I never did. The earth is part of my body, and I never gave up the earth." Howard in turn insisted "that the government has set apart a reservation, and that the Indians must go upon it."

Angered now, the Nez Perce chief turned directly to Howard. In a fierce and fiery voice, he asked, "What person pretends to divide the land, and put me on it?" To this Howard said, "I am that man. I stand here for the President, and there is no spirit good or bad that will hinder me. My orders are plain, and will be executed." Toohoolhoolzote said that the Indians wished to be left alone, warning Howard that white men were "trifling with the law of the earth." The chief concluded with a pronouncement that the treaty Nez Perce "may do what they like, but I am not going on the reservation."

Howard then completely lost his temper. "This bad advice is what you give the Indians," he exclaimed. "On account of it, you will have to be taken to the Indian Territory." The general threatened to "send [them] there if it takes years and years" and ordered one of his men, Captain David Perry, to arrest Toohoolhoolzote. The Nez Perce chief responded by asking, "Do you want to scare me in reference to my body?" to which Howard said, "I will leave your body with Captain Perry." The soldiers took Toohoolhoolzote across the parade grounds of Fort Lapwai to the guardhouse. Howard put the chief in jail while the others watched in silence.

The general returned to the council and asked each chief if he would move his band onto the reservation. Chief Joseph's nephew, Yellow Wolf, said that Howard had "showed the people the rifle," making it clear that their only alternative was to fight. Joseph himself described the situation by saying that Howard was like the grizzly bear and the Indians were like the deer. Sometime before the council, Ollokot, leader of the young warriors, had acknowledged the futility of fighting. "I have eyes and a heart," Ollokot said, "and can see and understand for myself that

Ollokot, the brother of Chief Joseph and leader of the young Nez Perce warriors, maintained at the Second Lapwai Council that battling the United States would be futile.

The Camas Prairie, located near the present-day town of Grangeville, Idaho. Shortly before the nontreaty Nez Perce were to report to the reservation in 1877, they gathered at this old meeting ground for their last taste of freedom.

if we fight we would have to leave all and go into the mountains. I love my wife and children and could not leave them." Like Ollokot, none of the other leaders wanted war, so one by one each agreed to move.

Before the Indians left the council, Howard gave each band a letter that gave them the government's official permission to travel across the plateau.

If settlers tried to prevent their movement to the reservation, the Indians were to give them the general's letter. Howard told the chiefs to have their people on the reservation in 30 to 35 days. This deadline was a hardship for the people. They quickly had to sell or pack their goods and gather their horses and cattle together for the journey. Their animals grazed freely, so the

rivers, and valleys. The people had a spiritual relationship to these sites and the earth that held the bones of their parents, grandparents, and children. As the people departed, they wept because they were leaving a part of themselves behind.

Before moving onto the reservation, the Nez Perce came together on the Camas Prairie near present-day Grangeville, Idaho. The wide-open prairie was an old gathering place for the people. They raced horses and gathered nutritious roots there. In the spring the prairie blossomed with a beautiful blanket of purple flowers, the blooms of camas plants, the bulbs of which were a potatolike vegetable. The mountains rose along the horizon, and pine trees dotted the expansive landscape. Meeting on the Camas Prairie, the Nez Perce had one final taste of the liberty and freedom that they had known since the beginning of time. But the Law set down at creation was about to change. No longer would the people be allowed to hunt, gather, fish, travel, or worship without the watchful eye of the Bureau of Indian Affairs. Their days as free people had been destroyed by the United States. ▲

roundup took time. Even more difficult was saying good-bye to their homeland. Contained within the boundaries of the Nez Perce country were numerous sacred sites—mountains, hills,

Chief Moses, photographed in the late 19th century. An advocate of peace, Moses raised a war party during the Nez Perce War to protect his people from a volunteer force led by Colonel Enoch Pike but was able to avoid a battle with Pike's men.

THE
NEZ PERCE
WAR

While the Indians camped at Camas Prairie, an event occurred that brought forth all the fury the Nez Perce had felt since the signing of the Thief Treaty. A young man named Wahlitits purposely allowed his horse to trample some camas that a women had laid out to dry in the sun. She and her husband scolded Wahlitits, saying that if he wanted to pretend to be a great warrior, he should avenge the death of his father, Eagle Robe. Eagle Robe had been murdered the previous year by Larry Ott, a white settler. With his dying breath, he had asked his son not to retaliate. But after the scolding, Wahlitits decided he could no longer obey his father's wishes. With two other young men, Swan Necklace and Red Moccasin Tops, Wahlitits set out to kill Ott.

The three Indians first raided several white settlements along the Salmon River. Although they could not find Ott, they came upon other whites who had harassed their people. They killed three men and wounded another. When news of the Indians' actions became known, the young men of Nez Perce chief White Bird's band formed a war party. The result was more violence and an outcry by whites against all of the Nez Perce. The leaders had tried hard to avoid war by agreeing to leave their homes. They could do nothing, however, to reverse the hostile actions of Wahlitits and his friends.

When word reached the Nez Perce camped at the Camas Prairie, the Indians met in council to talk about their course of action. They knew that Howard would probably send troops to engage them, but they still held out the hope that the soldiers would want to negotiate peace rather than fight a prolonged war. The chiefs decided to move south to White Bird Canyon, where they could intercept the troops. If the soldiers came to fight rather than talk, the Indians would be in a good position to defend themselves.

Soon Captain Perry rode into White Bird Canyon with a combined force of regular and volunteer soldiers. The Nez Perce never had a chance to negotiate a peace. Shots rang out almost immediately, and the fight was on. The army suffered heavy losses and the Nez Perce drove them out of the canyon. Fighting continued along the Salmon River. A few treaty Nez Perce had joined forces with the army, so treaty and nontreaty Indians found themselves squared off against each other.

Confusion reigned among the Nez Perce at the outset of the war. They had not planned on the conflict, and they moved about the region of the Salmon River trying to determine what to do. Eventually they congregated at Weippe Prairie, where they met to discuss their next course of action.

By this time, they had been joined by Young Looking Glass (the son of Old Looking Glass, who had signed the Nez Perce Treaty of 1855). He had been hunting east of the Bitterroot Mountains when the war began. Howard sent his troops on an unprovoked attack of the chief's village, which drove Looking Glass and his people into the fold of the hostile Nez Perce.

Many of the Indians listened to Looking Glass's advice. The chief was about 45 years old, and he had distinguished himself as a brave and capable warrior on the Great Plains. He had successfully fought the Sioux and was of the buffalo-hunting class. In council he told the Nez Perce leaders that they should retreat over the Bitterroot Mountains by way of the Lolo Trail. He reasoned that if the Indians departed the region, they would leave their troubles behind them.

The Indians followed the chief over the rugged terrain of the Bitterroot Mountains. Howard and his troops pursued the Nez Perce, but they could not catch them. Some volunteer soldiers stationed near present-day Missoula, Montana, then assembled at the eastern edge of the Lolo Trail. They set up a crude fort from which to fight and planned on preventing the Nez Perce from moving forward. When the Indians appeared, however, the soldiers, unseasoned and outnumbered, decided not to fight and allowed Looking Glass and the others to move through the area. Montanans later nicknamed the volunteers' barricade "Fort Fizzle."

After the Nez Perce moved into the Bitterroot Valley of Montana, they had an avenue of escape open to them. With ease, they could have turned north through the valley and passed through the villages of the Flathead and into Canada. They chose not to, however, believing they had escaped the soldiers. Looking Glass and others believed that the United States only wanted them off their homelands. In council, the Indians decided to travel south and east onto the plains of Wyoming and Montana, where they could hunt buffalo. Looking Glass knew this territory well, and he believed he had friends among the Crow Indians. The leaders followed Looking Glass south to the Big Hole, a valley in Montana.

Young Looking Glass, the son of the great war chief Old Looking Glass, who signed the Treaty of 1855. The young chief and his people were drawn into the Nez Perce War of 1877 by General Howard's unprovoked attack on their village.

A sketch of the site of the Battle of the Big Hole. Resting after two months of travel over rugged terrain, the Nez Perce who had camped at the Big Hole were unprepared for the brutal U.S. Army attack led by Colonel John Gibbon.

The Nez Perce arrived at the Big Hole in August. For two months they had been moving rapidly over the Bitterroot Mountains and through the rugged terrain of Idaho and Montana. They had fought several tough skirmishes and a few pitched battles. The band included several women, some of whom had fought alongside the warriors. The women had also nurtured their families through the arduous journey and had watched over and cared for the children. The women administered to the sick and wounded, serving as doctors and nurses. They also took care of the camp, pitching the tipis and cooking for everyone. Without them the men could not have moved so efficiently over the rugged terrain.

At the Big Hole River, the Indians rested. They fished, hunted, and cut new lodgepoles for their tipis. At night they told stories, sang, and danced. They did not celebrate a "victory," for they saw no victory in their flight or fight. Instead, they celebrated the time they had together in peace and quiet. Looking Glass believed that the Indians had outrun the army and that they had nothing to fear any longer. Some of the people objected to camping so long at the Big Hole, feeling that the soldiers might still be in pursuit. They wanted to move on, but others wanted to send their scouts back to determine if the soldiers had advanced. One Nez Perce, Wootolen, had a dream that the soldiers would attack, and he was known as a man of "strong powers." Still, Looking Glass maintained that the people had nothing to worry about. "All right, Looking Glass," Five Wounds, a Nez Perce warrior, said, "You are one of the Chiefs! I have no wife, no children to be placed fronting the danger that I feel coming to us. Whatever the gains, whatever the loss, it is yours."

On August 9, 1877, their worst nightmare came true. During the gray light of morning, the Palouse chief, Hahtalekin, walked from his tipi to check on his horses. He discovered the soldiers and sounded a warning. After briefly fighting the soldiers, he was shot dead. His son Five Fogs then came out of his lodge. According to Yellow Wolf, Five Fogs "was of an old time mind," even though he was "aged about thirty snows." He did not use a gun, but "was good with the bow." Yellow Wolf said, "If he had good rifle, he could bring death to the soldiers." However, Five Fogs "stood there shooting arrows at the enemies" until a bullet struck him. He died instantly.

The troops, under Colonel John Gibbon, had surprised the Nez Perce by crawling on their hands and knees until they were very close to the village. When the fight began, women and children rushed from their tipis, only to be met with a shower of bullets. Some soldiers inadvertently killed the women and children. Others shot them on purpose. Gibbon had told the soldiers that he did not want prisoners, so they shot everything that moved. One Nez Perce, Wounded Head, described the ugly

White Feather, a Nez Perce woman who survived the Battle of the Big Hole, said that the men, women, and children who died in the conflict "had not done wrong to be so killed. We had only asked to be left in our homes."

scene this way: "Hand to hand, club to club. All mixed up, warriors and soldiers fought. It was a bloody battle." Bullets fell like hail, ripping "the tepee walls, pattering like raindrops."

For 20 minutes the soldiers fought their way forward, until they took much of the camp. Eighty-nine tipis stood along the riverbanks. The soldiers transformed the serene scene into a bloody nightmare. They set fire to many lodges and slashed at the tipi walls. The warriors fought the soldiers as well as they could. When they were losing heart, one man named White Bird shouted, "Why are we retreating? Since the world was made, brave men fight for their women and children. Fight!" The Nez Perce renewed the fight, driving the soldiers out of the camp. The Indians charged Gibbon's men, pinning them down while the women, children, and elders returned to take down the camp and pack the horses. In the end, between 60 to 90 people—the majority of whom were women and children—lay dead. Many more were wounded. The survivors mourned as they quickly buried the casualties.

Chief Joseph led the people as they hastily prepared to leave the Big Hole. Meanwhile, the warriors continued to fight Gibbon's troops, and they overtook a mountain howitzer and mule train carrying 2,000 rounds of ammunition. They kept up the attack all day, pinning down the soldiers while their families escaped. When the people were far enough down the trail, the warriors ended the fight and joined their loved ones. No one said anything to Looking Glass. The silence was their message. Looking Glass no longer led the people, and the tribe now looked to another, Lean Elk, to guide them.

The Indians moved south and east. Along the way they skirmished with Howard's troops at Camas Meadows. The Nez Perce battled well before giving up the fight. They then moved forward, riding into Crow country. Looking Glass had boasted about his friendship with the Crow, but this tribe had no interest in inviting them into their camps. During the previous year, the Crow had served as scouts for General Custer. They did not want to cause themselves trouble with the United States by housing the renegades. The Nez Perce eluded soldiers under Colonel Samuel D. Sturgis along the Clear Fork River, but the warriors stood and fought his men at Canyon Creek.

When the Crow refused to join forces with the Nez Perce, the people decided to escape into Canada. Sitting Bull and some other Sioux had moved to Canada, and some people thought that the great chief might come to their aid. While the Nez Perce were making their plans, Howard made some of his own. After the Battle of Canyon Creek, Sturgis sent a soldier to Tongue River Cantonment with a message to Colonel Nelson A. Miles. Howard figured out that the Nez Perce planned to go to Canada, so he wanted Miles to cut off the Indian advance. With a force of about 400 men, including 30 Cheyenne

Nez Perce warriors seized this mountain howitzer and 2,000 rounds of ammunition from their enemy during the Battle of the Big Hole. The Indians dismantled the cannon and used the ammunition to hold off the troops while their families escaped from the battleground.

and Sioux scouts, Miles set off to intercept the Nez Perce.

Howard had not been able to capture the Nez Perce, and newspapers all over the country reported this fact. The war proved to be an embarassment for the army, particularly for General Howard and William Tecumseh Sherman—the commander of the U.S. Army. Throughout the campaign, Howard had told journalists that he would capture the Nez Perce. At one point, he declared that he would trap them "the day after tomorrow." He did not succeed, and thereafter the Nez Perce mocked Howard by nicknaming him The Day After Tomorrow.

During their trip north, Looking Glass regained his position of leadership. He knew that Howard's troops were days behind them but had no idea that Miles had been summoned to cut them off. The chief therefore advised the people to slow down and rest before crossing into Canada. Tired and wounded, the Nez Perce were eager to believe they had plenty of time.

By September 29, they reached Snake Creek, a tributary of the Milk River. The creek was situated between the Little Rocky Mountains and Bear Paw Mountains. The area offered a good place to rest, and the Indians decided to camp there for a few days. The

Nez Perce were 40 miles from the Canadian border—48 hours from freedom. While they rested, soldiers under Miles rode pell-mell toward their camp.

Through a miserable cold rain and thick fog, the Cheyenne and Sioux scouts found the Nez Perce. Shortly after bringing up his men, Miles attacked, and a bloody battle ensued. The Indians and soldiers fought at close range. The fighting often was hand-to-hand combat in which women and children fought off the soldiers with digging sticks and butcher knives. The Nez Perce warriors, now quite adept at firing their rifles, picked off several soldiers with dead accuracy. Miles lost so many men that he called off the charge. He ordered a siege of the Nez Perce camp. The weather grew worse. Soon five inches of snow lay on the ground, and the people suffered from hunger and exposure. But they continued to fight as patriots for their freedom.

On October 1, 1877, Miles raised a flag of truce and called out to Joseph. He wanted to meet the Nez Perce chief and talk terms of the Indians' surrender. The Nez Perce met among themselves first to decided what action to take. Missing from this important gathering were Ollokot, Toohoolhoolzote, and Lean Elk, all of whom had been killed during the first day of fighting. Looking Glass and White Bird worried about a cease-fire, saying that General Howard would hang them just as Colonel Wright had hanged the Indians following the Plateau Indian War of 1855–58. Tom Hill, a Nez Perce inter-preter, visited Miles and asked for his assurance that if Joseph came forward to talk, he would not be harmed. Miles agreed, saying that he would meet the Nez Perce chief halfway between the two camps.

Miles demanded an unconditional surrender whereby the Indians would lay down all of their arms. Joseph wanted his people to keep half of their weapons for hunting, but Miles balked at the idea. The talks ended on this note, but as Joseph was leaving, Miles ordered his soldiers to capture the chief. When they grabbed Joseph, the Indians took prisoner Lovell H. Jerome, a lieutenant who was visiting the Nez Perce camp. The soldiers then released Joseph, and the Indians allowed Jerome to go.

General Howard arrived at Bear Paws on October 5. On the same day, Meopkowit (Old George) and Jokais (Captain John)—two treaty Nez Perce who had scouted for the army—rode into the enemy camp to announce that Miles and Howard wanted "no more war!" This news provided the Nez Perce an honorable way to end the fighting, because the whites were asking for peace. As Yellow Wolf stated, "We were not captured. It was a draw battle." The Indians believed that they were agreeing to a conditional surrender whereby the warriors would not be punished for participating in the war. Also, they thought that they would be allowed to return to Idaho to live on the Nez Perce reservation. Joseph reported that Miles had said, "If you will come

THE NEZ PERCE WAR OF 1877

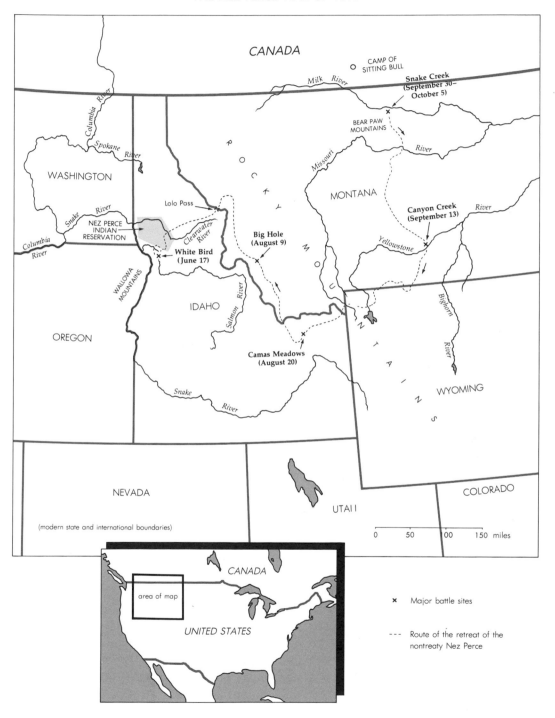

CANADA

CAMP OF
SITTING BULL

Snake Creek
(September 30–
October 5)

Milk River

BEAR PAW
MOUNTAINS

Columbia River

Spokane River

WASHINGTON

R
O
C
K
Y

Missouri

MONTANA

Canyon Creek
(September 13)

River

Bighorn River

Lolo Pass

Snake River

NEZ PERCE
INDIAN
RESERVATION

Clearwater River

Big Hole
(August 9)

M
O
U

Yellowstone

Columbia
River

White Bird
(June 17)

WALLOWA
MOUNTAINS

IDAHO

Salmon River

N
T
A
I
N
S

WYOMING

OREGON

Camas Meadows
(August 20)

Snake River

(modern state and international boundaries)

0   50   100   150 miles

NEVADA

UTAH

COLORADO

CANADA

area of map

UNITED STATES

✕   Major battle sites

- - -   Route of the retreat of the
         nontreaty Nez Perce

and give up your arms, I will spare your lives and send you back to the reservation.'' If the Indians had not believed Miles's words and that the whites were honorable, they probably would never have surrendered.

Some of the Nez Perce—including Yellow Wolf, Joseph's 12-year-old daughter, and White Bird—escaped to Canada. They made it safely, only to meet trouble while living with Sitting Bull's Sioux. Ollokot's wife was among those who left. Years later she spoke of the tragic night she left the others.

> Husband dead, friends buried or held prisoners. I felt that I was leaving all that I had but I did not cry. You know how you feel when you lose kindred and friends through sickness-death. You do not care if you die. With us it was worse. Strong men, well women, and little children killed and buried. They had not done wrong to be so killed. We had only asked to be left in our own homes, the homes of our ancestors. Our going was with heavy hearts, broken spirits. But we would be free. . . . All lost, we walked silently on into the wintry night.

However, most of the Nez Perce—more than 400—remained with Joseph and surrendered with him at sundown. The weather was terrible, and the army told the Nez Perce and their Palouse allies that they would spend the winter at Fort Keogh in Montana. This made sense to the Nez Perce, who knew that

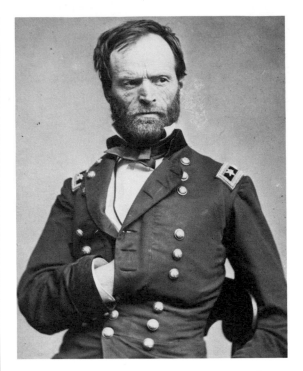

General William Tecumseh Sherman ignored the terms of the tribe's conditional surrender following the Nez Perce War. Instead of allowing the Indians to return to their Idaho reservation, Sherman ordered that they be taken to Fort Leavenworth, Kansas.

the Lolo Trail back to their country was blocked by snow. However, not long after arriving at Fort Keogh, Miles received orders to send the Nez Perce and the Palouse down the Yellowstone and Missouri rivers to Fort Lincoln near Bismarck, North Dakota. From there the Indians would be held as prisoners of war at Fort Leavenworth, Kansas. The soldiers took the Indians downriver on flatboats, and they arrived at Fort Leavenworth on November 27, 1877.

General William Tecumseh Sherman had changed the terms of the conditional surrender negotiated by Miles and Howard. Sherman was no friend to Indian people. In 1867, Sherman had said, "The more [Indians] we can kill this year, the less will have to be killed the next war, for the more I see of these Indians, the more convinced I am that they all have to be killed or be maintained as a species of paupers." Sherman is also attributed with the saying that the only good Indian is a dead Indian. Sherman wanted to push his heel into the Nez Perce, the people who had held off the army so effectively and garnered the admiration of many whites. He told General Philip Sheridan to remove the Nez Perce to Kansas, and the general gave the orders to Miles. The colonel had learned to respect the Nez Perce people, but he felt he had no choice but to do what he was told.

The 431 Indians held at Fort Leavenworth were wracked by depression, despair, and disease. Death stalked the Nez Perce during their eight-month stay along the banks of the Missouri River. Twenty-one people died. The Indians lived under deplorable conditions, and the army did little to ensure their survival. According to S.T.T., an unknown observer who visited the Nez Perce and wrote a letter to *Council Fire* [an obscure journal], "The 400 miserable, helpless, emaciated specimens of humanity, subjected for months to the malarial atmosphere of the river bottoms, presented a picture which brought to my mind the horrors of [the Civil War prison of] Andersonville." More than half the Indians—mostly women and children—became ill, suffering primarily from malaria.

In July 1878, the soldiers moved the Indians to their new home on the Quapaw Agency in Indian Territory. For a year the Nez Perce remained in present-day northeastern Oklahoma before the government moved them to the Ponca Agency in what is now Tonkawa, Oklahoma. Agent William H. Whiteman had not received food, clothing, medicine, or the resources to provide shelter for the new arrivals. He told the Indians that he "was utterly ignorant of the plans of the Department" to move the Nez Perce and the Palouse onto the Ponca Reservation. The outcome was predictable. Indians died from disease, malnutrition, and exposure. The Nez Perce hated Indian Territory and called it Eekish Pah, the Hot Place. Still, they made the best of their situation by ranching, farming, and worshiping at the Christian mission. However, Husishusis Kute continued to lead the people in Washani prayers, songs, and dances. Under his guidance, the people prayed for deliverance.

Joseph, Husishusis Kute, Yellow Bull, and the others did more than pray. Whenever possible, they met with government officials to present their case. Commissioner of Indian Affairs Ezra A. Hayt and the Board of Indian Commissioners investigated the Nez Perce's situation, but they did nothing to reverse Sherman's decision to exile the Indians. In January 1879, Joseph and Yellow Bull traveled to Washington, D.C., where they met with politicians and reporters. Joseph expressed his feelings, saying, "My heart is sad when I think of my home, which the Great Spirit gave my fathers." The whites listened but again did nothing. Politicians in the Northwest lobbied against the return of the Nez Perce, and the officials in the nation's capital listened to their pleas.

In March 1879, Joseph returned to Washington, D.C., where he made his case again. While there, he gave an interview to the *North American Review*, which appeared in the April issue under the title, "An Indian's View of Indian Affairs." Joseph described the history of his people and gave his interpretation of events that led to the war and surrender. Joseph said he did not believe that "the Great Spirit Chief gave one kind of a man the right to tell another . . . what to do." He said, "No man owned any part of the earth, and a man could not sell what he did not own." Joseph addressed the issue of American equality, saying that all people "were made by the Great Spirit Chief. They are all brothers. The earth is the mother of all people, and all people should have equal rights upon it." The article won Joseph great acclaim and focused national attention on the Nez Perce.

Joseph returned to the Hot Place sick in body and soul. He told the superintendent of Indian affairs for Oregon, A. B. Meacham, "You come to see me as you would a man upon his death-bed." He also told the superintendent that the Creator "has left me and my people to our fate" and that "death comes almost every day for some of my people." Death, he said, "will soon come for all of us." Joseph prophesied that the Nez Perce and the Palouse were "a doomed people" who would soon "be in the ground."

While Joseph worried about his people's fate, non-Indian reformers worked diligently to win their return to the Northwest. Women, particularly Christian women, organized efforts on behalf of the Nez Perce. In 1883, the Bureau of Indian Affairs allowed James Reuben, a Christian Nez Perce, to lead 33 women and children to the Nez Perce reservation in Idaho. One of the Nez Perce recorded that words could not "express our joy when we remembered that our feet will soon tread again on our native land, and our eyes behold the scenes of our childhood. The undying love for home, which we have cherished in our hearts so long, has caused our tears to flow for years."

On July 4, 1884, Senator Henry L. Dawes secured passage of a bill empowering the secretary of the interior to decide the fate of the Nez Perce. As a result, on April 29, 1885, Commissioner of Indian Affairs John D. Atkins ordered the return of the Nez Perce to the Northwest. The Indians signed away their holdings in Indian Territory and bid farewell to their loved ones who had died during their ordeal. By train they traveled to Wallula Junction, Washington Territory, where Special Agent W. H. Faulkner split the Nez

Yellow Bull, photographed in 1905. Along with Chief Joseph, Yellow Bull traveled to Washington, D.C., in January 1879 to meet with federal officials. The leaders pressed the politicians they met to allow the Nez Perce to leave Indian Territory, where disease, malnutrition, and exposure were taking the lives of their people, young and old.

Perce and the Palouse into two groups. Because of indictments against Joseph and others, the government forced Joseph and 150 Indians to stay and settle on the Colville Indian Reservation. Husishusis Kute and 118 people were removed to the Nez Perce reservation in Idaho. As a result, some of the participants of the Nez Perce War resettled in Idaho among the treaty Nez Perce; others resettled in Washington among Salish-speaking Indians.

The Nez Perce had returned to the Northwest, but most could not go back to their old homes. Some of Looking Glass's people returned to Idaho to live in or near their former homes. The bands of White Bird, Rainbow, Tohoolhoolzote, Husishusis Kute, and others could not reside on the lands that held the bones of their ancestors because these areas were now off the reservation. Some of the Indians ignored the government and moved back to their old homes, anyway.

The late 19th century was a time of continual turmoil for the Nez Perce people. The remembrances of one Nez Perce man, Andrew George, aptly illustrates the pain of their experiences during this period. Both his mother and father had fought in the war and had lived in Indian Territory. When he was a boy, his family moved to the village of Palus and later were removed by the U.S. Army to the Nez Perce reservation. As George grew up, his parents rarely spoke to him about the Hot Place, but when they did they wept for the men, women, and children who had lost their lives fighting for their freedom. About 431 Indians had arrived at Fort Leavenworth in 1877, but only 268 left the Hot Place 8 years later. George's people were among those who returned but could never forget this tragic era of Nez Perce history. ▲

A Nez Perce man performing a hoop dance in Yakima, Washington, in 1987.

REBIRTH
OF THE
PEOPLE

In the 1870s and 1880s, many white people traveled into the American West not to seek their fortune or a place to settle, but merely to see the sights. Included in many vacation specials was a visit to an Indian reservation where tourists could meet "real" Indians. The vacationers had a preconceived idea of what they would see. They imagined Indians with noble faces, wearing feathers and war paint while riding their ponies across the plains and prairies. What the travelers found instead were proud people suffering from malnutrition and disease. Many of them decided that the problem with Indians was the reservation system, which offered no incentive for Native Americans to get ahead. They reasoned that Indians did not have a stake in society because they did not own the land outright.

Several of these well-meaning whites returned to the East eager to "uplift" the Indians. Some of them set out to destroy the reservations and divide them into small tracts called allotments. Unlike reservation land, which was held in trust by the government on behalf of entire Indian groups, allotments would become the private property of individual Indians over time. These whites' line of reasoning held that if Indians owned their own land, they would work long and hard to make a good living from the earth. This reform appealed to many Christians who felt that private landownership would solve the so-called Indian problem.

Other Americans sided with the Christian reformers. They agreed that the reservations should be allotted, but for another reason. Western farmers, ranchers, merchants, miners, and others who lived near Indian peoples realized that Indians had a view of the earth that differed from that of white Americans. These opportunists knew that if the government broke up the reservations into individual plots, they would be able to buy Indian lands for practically nothing. The Nez Perce had done some farming and ranching. Yet, traditionally, their lives revolved around the seasonal round of fishing, hunting, and gathering. Since the beginning of time, they had lived principally along the rivers. Their permanent village sites remained their homes during the reservation era. The Indians used the fertile hills surrounding the rivers as grazing lands, but they did not farm the vast majority of these lands. Believing

they could purchase these areas cheaply, western farmers, ranchers, and others joined hands with the reformers to push the government to allot Indian land.

Senator Henry L. Dawes responded by drawing up an allotment bill and presenting it to Congress. Indians throughout the United States opposed Dawes's bill. Some Indians on the Nez Perce and Colville reservations voiced their concerns over the act. Even some

Nez Perce farmers at Camp Corbett in Idaho, photographed circa 1900. Many government officials and social reformers in the late 19th century believed that the widespread poverty of reservation Indians could be alleviated if they were given their own plots of land and encouraged to become farmers.

An early-20th-century photograph of Colville and Nez Perce residents of the Colville Indian Reservation in Washington. Although the Indians living on both the Colville and Nez Perce reservations were distressed by their poor living conditions, most were opposed to the General Allotment Act of 1887, which called for the division of their common land into small, individually owned tracts.

whites worried about what would happen if the bill was passed into law. For example, Senator Henry M. Teller prophesied that within 40 years the Indians would lose title to all their traditional lands and would "curse the hand that was raised professedly in their defense." And the House Committee on Indian Affairs reported that no matter what the humanitarians thought, an allotment act would not "make a farmer out of an Indian." The committee believed that "the real aim of this bill is to get at the Indian lands and open

them to settlement." The congressmen concluded their report in this way:

> If this were done in the name of greed, it would be bad enough; but to do it in the name of humanity and under the cloak of an ardent desire to promote the Indian's welfare by making him like ourselves, whether he will or not, is infinitely worse.

In spite of opposition from Indians and whites alike, the national government passed the General Allotment Act (also known as the Dawes Act) in 1887. The act allowed the executive branch to survey the Nez Perce and other tribes and to prepare tribal rolls in order to identify each Indian on the reservations. Each family head would secure 160 acres, and each single person—male or female—over 18 years of age and every orphan secured 80 acres. Children under 18 received an allotment of 40 acres. A government agent would assign allotments, and once they were done, no more allotments would ever be assigned. The government was to hold the title to each allotment for 25 years, during which time the land would be tax exempt. After this time, the land titles would be issued to the allottees. Indians who accepted the allotments were made citizens of the United States, but they were not automatically made citizens of the county and states in which they resided.

In 1889, Alice Fletcher, an anthropologist from Harvard University, accepted the assignment of allotting the Nez Perce reservation in Idaho. She asked the Nez Perce to help her in her work, and the Indians responded by appointing nine Nez Perce men—all Christian religious leaders—to act as representatives of the people from the different Indian communities. For four years Fletcher worked among the Nez Perce families, making a detailed study of the individuals living on the reservation. In 1893, the United States sent three agents to the Nez Perce reservation to negotiate an agreement whereby the Indians would accept allotment. By

the time these men arrived on the reservation, the Indians believed that they had to accept allotment. Many whites and some key Indian leaders—particularly Christian Indians who believed in progress through white "civilization"—favored the agreement.

Under the terms of the Nez Perce Allotment Agreement of 1893, the Indians ceded to the United States 542,000 acres. They kept their individual allotments and 34,000 acres that contained timber, buildings, and cemeteries. In return, the United States promised the Nez Perce $1,626,222, most of which would be paid in installments. The government was to make specific improvements on the reservation and to keep whites off of it until it issued land titles to the Indian allottees. On November 8, 1895, President Cleveland declared the agreement to be valid, and on November 18, the government opened all unallotted lands to white settlers.

Like the Nez Perce reservation in Idaho, the Colville reservation in Washington State was also allotted. The Nez Perce and the Palouse—both fairly recent arrivals at the Colville reservation—had little say in the matter. They took allotments near Nespelem, Washington, and stayed primarily among themselves.

The allotment of both the Nez Perce and Colville reservations proved disastrous for the Indians living there. The government passed subsequent legislation making it easier for whites to move onto reservation land and for Indians to sell their lands to whites. In general, Indians did not see the earth as something that could be bought or sold like a horse. To them, it could no more be sold than the air they breathed. When offered cash for their allotments, many took it to feed their loved ones. Some of them realized what they were doing; others did not. People permanently lost their lands, and they suffered as a result. More and more whites bought Indian lands, and thousands of acres fell out of Indian ownership and into the hands of non-Indian people. This happened everywhere in the United States among many of the tribes, including the Nez Perce of Idaho and Washington. However, the Nez Perce did better than many Indians in coping with allotment. Instead of losing all their territory like some Indian groups, much of their land remained in the hands of older tribal members.

From 1887 to 1934, the United States employed the General Allotment Act in its dealings with Native Americans. According to Arrell M. Gibson, a historian from the University of Oklahoma, the act "liquidated all of the reservations and nations of the 67 tribes of the Indian Territory, the lands of the northern Kickapoos and Potawatomis in Kansas . . . Nez Perces, and Spokanes." Gibson claims that in 1500 the Indians living in what is today the United States occupied 3 billion acres of land. In 1887, the Indians in the United States had 150 million acres. At the time the General Allotment Act was repealed in 1934, the Indians had "about 48 million acres, much of it desert."

Anthropologist Alice Fletcher accompanied surveyors to the Nez Perce Indian Reservation in 1893 in order to oversee the assignment of allotments. For four years, she worked on the reservation, making a detailed study of the people living there.

Nez Perce students at Carlisle Indian School in Pennsylvania. The government compelled many young Indians to attend schools operated by white educators so that they would learn English and assimilate into non-Indian society.

In some ways, the Nez Perce were isolated, but they were also a part of the larger world. The government forced them to send their children to the Indian school at Lapwai, Chemawa Indian School in Oregon, or Carlisle Indian School in Pennsylvania. White educators forced Indian children to speak English and to obey their commands. Americans tried to acculturate Indians through boarding schools, but the Indians resisted. Most children refused to surrender their culture altogether. Some Nez Perce assimilated, becoming more like non-Indians. For instance, they wore non-Indian clothing and ate non-Indian food. However, they re-

mained true to their people and held on to their language, culture, and beliefs.

When the United States entered World War I and World War II, Nez Perce men and women joined in the war effort. Some enlisted in the armed forces, serving at home and overseas. They also took jobs in defense plants and bought war bonds to help their country. These two world wars took many Nez Perce to foreign lands for the first time. The men and women fought for the United States, and some of them never came home. Each spring, the Nez Perce remember these people, as well as the Indians who died fighting for their way of life in the 19th century. In the spring of 1991, the Indians again remembered these people and honored their young men and women who had served their country in the Persian Gulf war.

As far as government systems are concerned, the Indians on the Nez Perce and Colville reservations had a long tradition of self-rule. They had functioned successfully for hundreds of years prior to white contact. Yet their forms of government did not have their roots in European tradition and therefore were little respected by Americans. With the signing of the Nez Perce Treaty of 1855, they came under the jurisdiction of the Bureau of Indian Affairs, which rarely consulted the Indians about their own desires and needs. However, the Indians eventually organized a system by which they would rule themselves on certain matters.

On the Nez Perce reservation, for example, the Indians had a tribal government. They had a general council composed of all adult men and women. From this body, they selected a Business Committee, which served as an executive body. In 1923, the Nez Perce wanted a representative form of government, so they organized a committee to look into the matter. The committee, under the leadership of Corbett Lawyer (a grandson of Chief Lawyer), drew up a five-year plan under which the Nez Perce would function and move toward greater self-rule. The plan called for tribal government, formal education, health systems, and tribal justice.

The Nez Perce Indian Home and Farm Association was an outgrowth of the committee, and it helped significantly to lead to economic self-determination. In 1923, the amount of allotted lands controlled by the Nez Perce was only about half of what they had held in 1893. The Indians were

A Nez Perce soldier who enlisted in the U.S. Army during World War I. In both World War I and World War II, many Nez Perce men and women supported the United States by either serving in the military or working in defense plants.

James Stuart helped Alice Fletcher survey reservation lands in the 1890s. He was also elected to a nine-member committee organized to draft a tribal constitution in 1926. Although the document has since been revised, it continues to influence tribal affairs.

aware of this and established the association to find jobs; start businesses, farms, and trades; give advice; and cope with changing economic conditions. The association functioned so efficiently that the people wanted even greater governmental control of their economic well-being.

On April 26, 1926, men and women from the Nez Perce reservation met to discuss the creation of the tribal constitution. The people elected a nine-member committee—including James Stuart, Jesse Paul, Corbett Lawyer, Silas D. Whitman, and Paul F. Corbett—to draft the document. The Nez Perce finalized their constitution on December 6 and sent it to the commissioner of Indian affairs a few days later. The commissioner approved it on October 22, 1927. According to one Nez Perce elder, although the constitution has been revised, the document guided the tribe with "a considerable amount of influence."

During the Great Depression of the 1930s, President Franklin D. Roosevelt and Commissioner of Indian Affairs John Collier advocated the passage of the Indian Reorganization Act of 1934. The act established new guidelines for tribal governments and reorganized the administration of tribal lands. It encouraged Indians to preserve their cultural and historical heritage. Although the Nez Perce leaders were eager to study the new administrative program set forth in the act, they did not elect to restructure their government according to the terms of the legislation. On November 17, 1934, the Nez Perce of Idaho voted 252–214 against the act, choosing not to become a tribe under the Indian Reorganization Act. Still, in 1948 the Indians worked with the federal government, restructuring their constitution and bylaws in order to create the Nez Perce Tribal Executive Committee.

Corbett Lawyer, then a respected Nez Perce elder, stated that there were many reasons for the rejection of the act. Some Indians feared that their lands would become communal property and that individuals would lose control over the use of their lands. Others feared that they would have to pay taxes on allotted lands. Several Nez Perce, particularly the Christian ones, opposed the act because it would usher in a return to the old tribal ceremonies and customs. The "progressive" Indians worried about the emergence of the old ways that might be contrary to Christian beliefs. Other Indians, notably descendants of Looking Glass, quietly and defiantly held on to the old ways. Each year, Looking Glass's de-

scendants gather in the forested mountains of Idaho to sing, pray, and renew their bonds with one another. They never surrendered the traditional beliefs of their people and continue to hold on to them today.

This was also true of some Nez Perce families on the Colville reservation. There, the descendants of Chief Joseph, Husishusis Kute, Yellow Wolf, Yellow Bull, and others still gather to pray, dance, and sing. They practice the Seven Drums Religion, a modern version of the Washani of the 19th century. In recent years the people built a new longhouse in Nespelem, Washington,

Nez Perce youths playing a game of football, photographed in Idaho in 1985. Organized sports are greatly enjoyed by Nez Perce adults and children alike on both reservations.

Two Nez Perces posing on the banks of the Clearwater River in clothing they and their families have designed and made to wear at powwows.

where they worship in the manner of their ancestors. The Nez Perce hold on to the old beliefs, but they are also a part of the larger Indian community today. Nez Perce children attend schools, participate in sports, and often ride in regional rodeos. Some of the Nez Perce continue their education, graduating from Washington State University, the University of Idaho, the University of Washington, and other institutions.

The Nez Perce and the Palouse have made a significant contribution to the Colville Tribal Council, working side by side with the Salish-speaking tribes of the reservation. Men and women of Nez Perce ancestry serve the community in many ways. They have supported efforts to improve the health, education, and financial situation of the tribes. Each year, the Nez Perce participate in the Trophy Pow Wow, All-Indian Rodeo, and Circle Celebration. The Trophy Pow Wow and Circle Celebration are competitive powwows where men, women, and children compete for money, prizes, and trophies for their dancing, drumming, and singing. The Nez Perce are an integral part of the Colville Confederated Tribes, and their people hold many important positions on and off the reservation.

The Nez Perce on the Colville reservation and those on the Idaho reservation have differences rooted in their pasts. However, they also have many similarities. Both treasure their history, culture, and language. They support educational programs to preserve the Nez Perce language and their tribal histories. In 1973, the Nez Perce Tribe of Idaho published *Noon Nee-Me-Poo: We, the Nez Perces*, a history of the people, written by Allen Slickpoo, Sr., and Deward E. Walker. In 1977, both groups celebrated the centennial of the Nez Perce War by striking a silver medal with a likeness of Chief Joseph. The Nez Perce continue to celebrate their relationship with the earth, holding annual salmon, root, and berry ceremonies. In the first week of May each year, the people at Lapwai host a Root Festival, and each August they host Pi-Nee-waus Days, a celebration that features war dances. Throughout the year the Nez Perce gather periodically to play traditional Indian games and race horses.

Organized sports are enjoyed by Nez Perce children and adults alike from both reservations. Men and women form softball and basketball leagues, and they watch their children play volleyball, football, and baseball. Girls and boys also participate in rodeos and fairs.

All Nez Perce also have a common interest in preserving their treaty rights to fish, hunt, and gather on and off the reservation. They have fought legal battles over these rights, and some Indians have been imprisoned for their efforts. Although the Nez Perce have compelled several courts to acknowledge their treaty rights, they still look to the first Indian Law when determining where to fish, hunt, and gather.

The Nez Perce people share other things as well. Most importantly, they share a common bond with one another as Nez Perce people. According to their legends, Coyote used the rich blood from the heart of the Kamiah Monster to create the Nez Perce, and he made these great people to last forever. The Nez Perce have always been survivors. Through the tragedies of the last 100 years the Nez Perce survived, and they will continue to survive. The Nez Perce people can look to their past with pride. At the same time they can look to the future, knowing that they can and will overcome whatever adversity comes their way. Coyote meant it to be that way in the beginning, and this is the way it will always be for the people known as the Nez Perce. ▲

BIBLIOGRAPHY

Brown, Mark. *The Flight of the Nez Perce.* Lincoln: University of Nebraska Press, 1967.

Haines, Francis. *The Nez Perces.* Norman: University of Oklahoma Press, 1955.

Howard, Oliver O. *Famous Indian Chiefs I Have Known.* New York: Century, 1907–8.

———. *My Life and Experiences Among Our Hostile Indians.* Hartford: Worthington, 1907.

———. *Nez Perce Joseph.* Boston: Lee and Shepard, 1881.

Young Chief Joseph. "An Indian's View of Indian Affairs." *North American Review* 128 (1879): 412–33.

Josephy, Alvin M., Jr. *The Nez Perce Indians and the Opening of the Northwest.* New Haven: Yale University Press, 1965.

McWhorter, Lucullus V. *Hear Me, My Chiefs!* Caldwell, ID: Caxton, 1952.

———. *Yellow Wolf: His Own Story.* Caldwell, ID: Caxton, 1940.

Ruby, Robert H., and John A. Brown. *Indians of the Pacific Northwest.* Norman: University of Oklahoma Press, 1982.

Slickpoo, Allen P., Sr., and Deward E. Walker, Jr. *Noon Nee-Me-Poo.* Lapwai, ID: Nez Perce Tribe of Idaho, 1973.

Trafzer, Clifford E., and Richard D. Scheuerman. *Renegade Tribe: The Palouse Indians and the Invasion of the Inland Pacific Northwest.* Pullman: Washington State University Press, 1986.

Wood, Henry Clay. *Status of Young Joseph and His Band of Nez Perce Indians and Supplementary to the Report on the Treaty Status of Young Joseph.* Portland, OR: Assistant Adjutant General's Office, Department of the Columbia, 1878.

THE NEZ PERCE AT A GLANCE

TRIBE   *Nez Perce*

CULTURE AREA   *Plateau*

GEOGRAPHY   *Eastern Washington, eastern Oregon, western Idaho*

CURRENT POPULATION   *Approximately 3,500*

FIRST CONTACT   *Meriwether Lewis and William Clark, American, 1805*

FEDERAL STATUS   *The Nez Perce Tribe of Idaho is recognized by the federal government. The Nez Perce living on the Colville Indian Reservation in Washington State are members of the Colville Confederated Tribes, which is recognized by the federal government.*

GLOSSARY

agent A person appointed by the Bureau of Indian Affairs to supervise U.S. government programs on a reservation and/or in a specific region. After 1908 the title *superintendent* replaced *agent*.

allotment U.S. policy applied nationwide through the General Allotment Act of 1887, aimed at breaking up tribally owned reservations by assigning individual farms and ranches to Indians. Allotment was intended as much to discourage traditional communal activities as to encourage private farming and assimilate Indians into mainstream American life.

anthropology The study of the physical, social, and historical characteristics of human beings.

assimilation The complete absorption of one group into another group's cultural tradition.

band A loosely organized group of people who are bound together by the need for food and defense, by family ties, and/or by other common interests.

Bureau of Indian Affairs (BIA) A U.S. government agency now within the Department of the Interior. Originally intended to manage trade and other relations with Indians, the BIA today seeks to develop and implement programs that encourage Indians to manage their own affairs and to improve their educational opportunities and general social and economic well-being.

civilization program U.S. policy of the 19th and early 20th centuries designed to change the Indians' way of life so that it resembled that of non-Indians. These programs usually focused on converting Indians to Christianity and encouraging them to become farmers.

culture The learned behavior of humans; nonbiological, socially taught activities; the way of life of a group of people.

General Allotment Act An act passed by U.S. Congress in 1887 that provided for the division of Indian reservations into individually owned tracts of land.

Indian Civilization Act An act passed by Congress in 1819 that allocated $10,000 of federal money for Indian education. Missionaries were encouraged to request money from this fund and use it to open schools for Indian students.

Indian Removal Act A bill passed by Congress in 1830. It authorized the president to set aside land west of the Mississippi River to which eastern tribes could be relocated, or removed. According to the terms of the act, no tribe could be removed against its will.

Indian Reorganization Act (IRA) The 1934 federal law that ended the policy of allotting plots of land to individuals and encouraged the development of reservation communities. The act also provided for the creation of autonomous tribal governments.

Indian Territory An area in the south central United States to which the U.S. government wanted to resettle Indians from other regions, especially the eastern states. In 1907, this area and Oklahoma Territory became the state of Oklahoma.

Manifest Destiny The belief in the 19th century that the United States had a God-given right to expand its borders to the Pacific Coast.

mission A religious center founded by advocates of a particular demonination who are trying to convert nonbelievers to their faith.

missionaries Advocates of a particular religion who travel to convert nonbelievers to their faith.

myth A story of an event of the prehistoric past. Myths often explain a practice, belief, or natural phenomenon.

parfleche French for "rawhide"; also, a folded rectangular container made of rawhide, used for storing dried foods, blankets, and clothing.

powwow An Indian social gathering that includes feasting, dancing, rituals, and arts and crafts displays, to which other Indian groups as well as non-Indians are now often invited.

removal policy A federal policy of the early 19th century that called for the sale of all Indian land in the eastern United States and the migration of Indians from these areas to lands west of the Mississippi River.

reservation, reserve A tract of land retained by Indians for their own occupation and use. *Reservation* is used to describe such lands in the United States; *reserve*, in Canada.

self-determination The federal government's current Indian policy, which gives tribes freedom to choose whether to remain on reservations, to form tribal governments, and to assume responsibility for services traditionally provided by the BIA.

tipi A conical, portable shelter made of poles and covered with buffalo hides.

treaty A contract negotiated between representatives of the U.S. government or another national government and one or more Indian tribes. Treaties dealt with the cessation of military action, the surrender of political independence, the establishment of boundaries, terms of land sales, and related matters.

tribe A society consisting of several or many separate communities united by kinship, culture, language, and other social institutions including clans, religious organizations, and warrior societies.

wyakin A guardian spirit power believed to come to Indian children during vigils to reveal truths about life and teach them special songs.

INDEX

PICTURE CREDITS

Photograph by Jim Baker, courtesy of Laboratory of Anthropology, University of Idaho, page 12; The Bettmann Archive, page 25; Big Hole National Battlefield/Photographer Jock Whitworth, page 85; The Denver Public Library, Western History Department, page 60; Historical Photograph Collections, Washington State University Libraries, pages, 64, 66, 75; Idaho Historical Society, pages 22 (neg. # 63-221.18), 34–35 (neg. # 684), 53 (bottom), 62 (neg. # 72-131.161), 76–77 (neg. # 696), 84 (neg. # 22866), 94 (neg. # 63-221.65), 97 (neg. # 63-221.24); Independence National Historic Park Collection, pages 14, 15; Library of Congress, pages 58, 88; Montana Historical Society, Helena, pages 82, 83; National Museum of American Art, Washington, D.C./Art Resource, NY, page 30; Nez Perce National Historical Park Collection, cover, pages 26, 49, 50 (left and right), 51 (top and bottom), 52, 53 (top), 54 (top and bottom), 55; Ohio Historical Society, page 56; Oregon Historical Society, pages 28 (cat. # 79073), 72 (cat. # 11275); Pacific University, Forest Grove, Oregon, page 33; Russell Lamb Photography, pages 92, 101, 102; Slickpoo Collection, pages 19, 38, 98, 99, 100; Smithsonian Institution, pages 17 (photo no. 2977), 57 (photo no. 2923-A), 81 (photo no. 2953-A); Special Collections Division, University of Washington Libraries, photo by Edward H. Latham, pages 20 (neg. # NA1009), 37 (neg. # 3436), 68 (neg. # UW12361), 70-71 (neg. # NA1294), 78 (neg. # NA948), 91 (neg. # NA1007), 95 (neg. # NA1301); Washington State Historical Society, Tacoma, Washington, pages 40, 42, 43, 45.
Maps (pages 2, 46, 87) by Gary Tong.

CLIFFORD E. TRAFZER, a member of the Wyandot Indian tribe, is professor and chair of ethnic studies and director of American Indian studies at the University of California, Riverside. He is the author of several books and articles on American Indian history and the coauthor of the award-winning *Renegade Tribe: The Palouse Indians and the Invasion of the Inland Pacific Northwest.*

FRANK W. PORTER III, general editor of INDIANS OF NORTH AMERICA, is director of the Chelsea House Foundation for American Indian Studies. He holds a B.A., M.A., and Ph.D. from the University of Maryland. He has done extensive research concerning the Indians of Maryland and Delaware and is the author of numerous articles on their history, archaeology, geography, and ethnography. He was formerly director of the Maryland Commission on Indian Affairs and American Indian Research and Resource Institute, Gettysburg, Pennsylvania, and he has received grants from the Delaware Humanities Forum, the Maryland Committee for the Humanities, the Ford Foundation, and the National Endowment for the Humanities, among others. Dr. Porter is the author of *The Bureau of Indian Affairs* in the Chelsea House KNOW YOUR GOVERNMENT series.